AROUND THE WORLD IN FAMILY DAYS

What We Learned When We Left It All Behind And Travelled the Globe

CHARLES ACHAMPONG

Lucky Book Publishing

To my incredible wife, Janice
thank you for making our life a beautiful adventure,
always pushing me to dream beyond what's
comfortable and embracing life to its fullest.

To my daughters, Kasia and Ayana
my playful explorers, who fill my life with
happiness and wonder.

And to my parents, George and Carol, who showed
me the world was meant to be explored.

I'm forever grateful for the journey that
began with all of you.

MY GIFT TO YOU

I am so glad you're here!

As my Gift to you, get FREE Access to the Audiobook of
Around the World in Family Days
by scanning the QR Code below or visiting
https://www.charlesachampong.com/thebook

TABLE OF CONTENTS

MY DREAM

My dream for this book is deeply personal. I want these pages to spark something in you—perhaps a realization that the barriers you perceive as too daunting are more surmountable than you think, or maybe a recognition that the "safe" path isn't always the richest one.

Through the story of our family's sabbatical, I want to show you the power of pausing and the clarity it can bring to your life. This isn't about abandoning your responsibilities. It's about discovering what becomes possible when you break from routine and give yourself room to breathe.

Whether you're reading this in a busy office dreaming of change or already planning your own adventure, I hope this book inspires you. Let it spark conversations about redefining success, finding growth in discomfort, and discovering that life's richest experiences often lie just beyond what we believe is possible.

If this speaks to you, I'd love your help in spreading it further. Whether you're planning an event, looking for a keynote speaker, or simply wanting to share this message, reach out. I'd be honoured to engage with audiences ready to pause, reflect, and dream bigger. Together, we can inspire others to live life with greater intention.

Because sometimes the bravest thing we can do is give ourselves permission to pause and envision the extraordinary.

http://www.charlesachampong.com

PROLOGUE

"Travelling – it leaves you speechless,
then turns you into a storyteller."
– Ibn Battuta

Travel isn't just about hopping from one place to another. It's been my greatest teacher long before I took my first steps. My first trip happened when I was nine months old. My Mom, who had a bit of wanderlust herself, took me to Trinidad and Tobago to visit my Uncle Herbie, a professor there. Of course, I don't remember, but apparently, I surprised my Dad when we returned by showing off my newfound walking ability. Looking back, it feels like that first adventure set the tone for everything that would follow.

Growing up, my love for travel was nurtured by family trips, though not always the kind I wanted. Every five years, we'd make the long, expensive journey from Canada to Ghana, where my family's roots lie, to visit relatives. I used to complain—why couldn't we go to Disneyland like my friends? My Dad would say, with his classic logic, "Don't worry; Ghana is exactly like Disney except for the rides, theme parks, and Mickey Mouse." That's pretty much like saying a bicycle is exactly like a car minus the engine, wheels, and steering wheel. But you know what? In his wonderfully wrong way, he was right—Ghana had its own kind of magic, just with fewer mouse ears.

Now I see those reluctant trips to Ghana were teaching me something valuable: there's power in stepping off the beaten path. While everyone else chased Mickey Mouse and magical castles, I was unknowingly exploring a different kind of story—one that would teach me the importance of charting my own course.

Then came the road trips across Canada, especially through the Atlantic provinces. Less exotic than Ghana, maybe, but just as meaningful. I'll never forget white-knuckling it through my first major drive—fresh licence in hand, steering our van across the Confederation Bridge to Prince Edward Island in the middle of a storm. My Dad, ever the educator, called it a 'teachable moment' in resilience. There I was, literally holding my entire family's fate in my hands as I inched our way across that 13 kilometre (8 mile) bridge, terrified but somehow thrilling in the adventure of it all.

Every trip, whether it was just a quick hop to a nearby town or a cross-country journey, made my world a little bigger, showing me just how many places were out there waiting to be discovered.

These family adventures laid the groundwork, but it wasn't until university that travel became more than just our family tradition. Working at the International Development Research Centre during Kofi Annan's time as United Nations Secretary-General changed everything for me. Seeing him—a man from Ghana, my ancestral home—rise to such global influence filled me with pride and opened my eyes. Suddenly, I saw how interconnected our world really was, and I couldn't ignore this pull to engage with the world on a larger scale.

That pull led me to Denmark for a semester abroad. What a change of scenery from growing up in Ottawa— I suddenly found myself surrounded by people who looked nothing like me. Gone were Ottawa's government buildings and monuments, replaced by bright row houses, green spaces, and bold modern designs. But it was there, surrounded by towering blond and blue-eyed Danes, that I really got what cultural exchange meant. Being the outsider taught me about truly embracing differences, not just observing them. As I bounced around Europe and northern Africa during that time—from Rome's ancient streets to Marrakech's buzzing souks—I started to see how the world was packed with stories. Stories I wanted to hear, live, and someday share.

By graduation, the travel bug had bitten me hard. While my friends were settling into comfortable government jobs in Ottawa, I felt pulled toward something less predictable. So I packed my bags for the last place anyone expected: Uganda, the Pearl of Africa. That year, working with the United Nations and Uganda Human Rights Commission, changed me in ways I'm still discovering.

Uganda wasn't just another stamp in my passport— it was where I really had to wrestle with real-world challenges and understand just how complex things could be. For the first time, I was in Africa without my family safety net. Sure, I looked like many people around me, but everything else was foreign—the stories, the struggles, and all those subtle cultural cues I was just beginning to pick up on.

I knew I wanted more of these experiences, and going back to school seemed like the right next step. That decision landed me in Vancouver for my MBA, where those gorgeous mountains and ocean views came with an unexpected bonus—meeting Janice, my future wife. Like me, she had this fire for exploration, and we instantly clicked over our shared dream of seeing the world beyond the usual tourist trails.

After working together at the Vancouver 2010 Olympics, we took the plunge—a three-month backpacking adventure through Southeast Asia. Navigating Bangkok's chaos, Cambodia's peaceful temples, and Laos's rugged landscape together, I knew I'd found my life partner. If we could handle the ups and downs of travel together, we could handle anything. Those three months didn't just strengthen our bond—they showed us we shared the same vision for a life full of adventure.

Life kept unfolding in the best way possible, leading to a beautiful wedding surrounded by loved ones celebrating our journey. Then we were off to Brazil for our honeymoon—a country bursting with colour, rhythm, and life. Standing at Christ the Redeemer in Rio, we watched an elderly man with an oxygen tank struggling up that steep path to the summit. It hit us hard—travel is a privilege that not everyone gets to experience. That's when Janice started musing about taking our future kids on a round-the-world trip. I remember thinking I'd just humour her—we were on our honeymoon after all—but a part of me wondered: is she crazy? Looking back now, that wild honeymoon dream set something in motion.

Our kids got their first taste of travel with winter trips to see their grandparents in Mexico, where they discovered the joy of tacos and endless sunshine. Our daughter Kasia took her first steps on Istanbul's streets, where locals called her 'the most beautiful hybrid baby' they'd ever seen (interesting choice of words, right?). When our family grew, so did our adventures—Croatia for Ayana's first trans-Atlantic journey, where she marveled at the crystal-clear waters of the Adriatic Sea.Then came Argentina and Uruguay, where the girls experienced their first glimpse of South America, dancing to tango music in the streets of Buenos Aires and sampling dulce de leche at every opportunity.

When I think about those family trips now, I can't help but trace it all back to that moment in Rio, watching that determined man with his oxygen tank. That seed of an idea would take over a decade to bloom into our journey around the world. We had no idea then how choosing adventure would shape our family's story.

From my first steps in Trinidad to watching my own kids discover the world, I've learned something important: while my story might be marked by passport stamps and plane tickets, the real lessons aren't about miles covered. They're about having the courage to step away from what's comfortable, even just for a moment, to see life through fresh eyes.

Maybe you're reading this thinking your life is too settled, too planned out, or too busy for adventure.

I get it.

But here's the beautiful truth I've discovered: sometimes the most extraordinary journeys don't require crossing oceans.

They begin in those small moments when we dare to break from our routines—whether it's through a sunrise walk in your own neighborhood, a weekend of complete disconnect, or simply choosing an unfamiliar path home.

This book carries the stories and lessons from our travels, but more than that, it's an invitation to discover your own path to wonder. My hope is that by the time you turn the final page, something will have shifted inside you— a spark of possibility, a whisper of courage, a desire to seek out your own adventures, whatever shape they may take. Because I've learned that life's most profound experiences rarely start with perfect plans. They start with a simple choice: to pause, to look up, to step off your usual path, and to let yourself be surprised by what you might find.

Your next chapter is waiting.

All you have to do is begin.

Charles Achampong

CHAPTER #1
LEAP INTO THE UNKNOWN

"Life is either a daring adventure or nothing at all."
– Helen Keller

I never intended to write a book. Honestly, who sits down one day and thinks, 'You know what would be fun? Let's pack up the family, travel the world, AND write about it.' Yet here I am, sharing our story of how we untangled ourselves from our carefully constructed life.

We'd always been the type to dream about extended travel—even had a dedicated savings account for it. But let's be real: I viewed it more as a 'nice idea' fund than an actual plan. Like saying you'll learn Italian or finally master sourdough bread—pandemic notwithstanding. Sure, we'd talk about it, scheme about it in that abstract way you plan for things you don't really expect to happen. The savings account was my way of playing along, a gesture that said 'see, I'm taking this seriously' while secretly thinking it would remain safely in the realm of someday.

Each trip we managed to squeeze in brought us closer, whether we were hopelessly lost in a new city or stumbling upon some place that wasn't in any guidebook. But these were always safely contained adventures — two weeks here, three weeks there. The idea of actually packing up our lives for an extended journey? That lived in a different realm of possibility entirely. There's something comforting about dreaming big while your routine stays perfectly intact.

Which I guess is the story of all our lives - isn't it?

But then life did what life does best—it got comfortable.

Really comfortable.

Our days became a blur of work deadlines, school drop-offs, and extracurricular activities. You know that feeling when you wake up one day and realize you're living on autopilot? That's when that distant dream started to shift from a pleasant someday fantasy to something more insistent. It wasn't discontent exactly—we had a good life, a really good life—but there was this nagging sense that we were capable of more, of something different.

After the kids were tucked in bed, Janice and I would sit on the couch, voices lowered, discussing the possibilities. Planning this adventure was equal parts terrifying and thrilling. We'd lie awake at night wrestling with questions that seemed to multiply:

Were we completely insane to pull the kids out of school?

Would our careers survive?

Would we?

Our late-night conversations ping-ponged between excited planning and mild panic attacks. But something about the idea of experiencing the world together as a family just wouldn't let go.

The planning phase revealed how much our thinking had evolved. What started as casual 'wouldn't it be nice' conversations had somehow shifted into 'how could we actually do this?' moments. It wasn't a sudden change— more like a slow awakening to the possibility that this crazy idea might not be so crazy after all. Each time we revisited the conversation, the questions became less about 'if' and more about 'when.' The dream had quietly moved from the realm of fantasy to something that felt within reach, even if the path wasn't entirely clear. Our talks became deeper, more purposeful, as we realized we weren't just entertaining an idea anymore—we were actually considering upending our entire lives for a short period of time for this adventure.

Let's be clear—we weren't delusional enough to think travelling would magically transform us into some perfect, Instagram-worthy family. My snoring would still drive everyone crazy, our kids would still bicker, and Janice would still give me that knowing look when I made questionable decisions. We decided to set our expectations so low that even a Cirque du Soleil performer would struggle to limbo under them. The goal wasn't perfection; it was simply being open to whatever lessons came our way.

Late at night, we'd huddle over our laptop, imagining our girls discovering bustling markets in Thailand, hiking through New Zealand's mountains, and finding pristine beaches in the Philippines. But here's the thing that kept us grounded—we knew how incredibly lucky we were to even consider this. This wasn't just about escaping the daily grind; it was about figuring out what was missing in our pretty comfortable lives. We had good jobs, a nice home, wonderful friends—yet something was pulling us toward a different kind of life experience.

The fear of the unknown is real. Questions about money, job security, and leaving everything familiar behind can freeze you faster than a Canadian winter. Through all our hushed conversations, we realized something: this wasn't about being fearless—it was about acknowledging all those fears and deciding to move forward anyway. Each small decision—from researching travel insurance to talking with the girls' teachers—felt like tiny steps toward making this dream tangible.

I've learned that the universe has this way of conspiring to help once you actually commit to something.

We wanted our girls to understand this—and that dreams don't just magically happen. They take work, planning, and usually a healthy dose of 'what are we thinking?' Sometimes the hardest part isn't the planning or the doing—it's making that initial decision to stop treating something as a fun fantasy and start treating it as a real possibility.

This book isn't just about our travels—though there are plenty of stories about navigating unfamiliar cities, attempting to order food with hand gestures, and those moments of cultural confusion that taught us more about ourselves than any guidebook could. It's about that moment when you realize your comfortable life might actually be a little too comfortable. It's about discovering what happens when you finally decide to turn those late-night dreams into reality. Our story is messy, imperfect, and real—just like any good adventure should be. Here's to our story, but more importantly, here's to inspiring you to write your own, whatever that may be.

The section at the end of each chapter serves a specific purpose. It is designed as an intentional stopping point—moments for readers to step away from my story and consider their own journey. Just as I learned the value of pausing through travel, these sections create space for readers to examine their lives, challenge their assumptions, and imagine new possibilities.

Each section includes key takeaways that distill the chapter's core messages, followed by insightful questions that encourage deeper personal reflection to be woven into actionable insights that you can apply to your daily life. This is an invitation to explore how the themes from each chapter might resonate with your own life circumstances, regardless of your specific situation.

Think of these sections as an opportunity for you to pause, breathe, and consider how to apply these lessons to your own journey of transformation.

Please share your journey and take the questions and reflections from each chapter and post your experiences on LinkedIn, Instagram, or Facebook using **#aroundtheworldifd**. Show how you're turning those ideas into action — your story could be exactly what someone else needs to hear to begin their own journey.

Key Takeaways

1. The Dream to Reality Shift: Moving from those casual "wouldn't it be nice" conversations to "wow, we might actually do this" moments. It wasn't some dramatic lightning bolt of inspiration — just quiet late-night talks that slowly turned our someday dream into a real possibility.

2. The Comfort Zone Paradox: Realizing you can be genuinely happy with your life and still feel pulled toward something different. It's that strange moment when you understand that wanting change isn't about escaping—it's about growing, even when things are pretty darn good.

3. The Reality of Being Brave: Understanding that courage isn't about being fearless or crazy confident. It's about having all those midnight doubts, acknowledging the scary parts, and still thinking "you know what? Let's give this a shot anyway."

Key Questions

1. What are you waiting for 'the right time' to do, and what small step could you take toward it now?

2. How can I bring a sense of adventure into my everyday life, even in small ways?

3. What's a dream or goal I have that feels big and scary, but exciting enough to be worth the risk?

PAUSE & REFLECT: Taking Your Own Leap

1. Start Small, Dream Big

    TODAY: Identify three routines in your life that feel stale and write down one small way to refresh each one—it could be as simple as taking a new route to work

    THIS WEEK: Choose one area of your life where you feel stuck and experiment with three different approaches to shake things up. Notice how each change, however small, affects your perspective

    THIS MONTH: Create a "curiosity calendar"—schedule one new experience each week that pushes you slightly out of your comfort zone

2. Face Your Fears

    *   List your top three immediate concerns about achieving your dream (e.g: fear of failure, fear of the unknown, fear of judgment)

    *   Design one small action step to address each concern

    *   Talk to someone who's made a similar change about how they overcame their fears

3. Take Ownership of Your Choice

    *   Block out two hours for deep reflection on what's holding you back

    *   Write out the cost of not making this change — both short and long term

    *   Create a weekly ritual that reinforces your commitment to change

CHAPTER #2
PREPARATION AND PLANNING:
THE ROAD TO DEPARTURE

"The greatest legacy we can leave our children
is not just our genes, but our hearts and minds
unafraid to break free from convention."
– Maya Angelou

While the idea of embracing adventure sounds appealing, the practical side of making it happen was a whole different story. Planning an extended journey around the world with my family required an attention to detail—something I'm not exactly known for. Thankfully, my spouse has those skills in abundance. From saving money and handling logistics to packing and choosing our destinations, the months leading up to our departure were filled with both excitement and a few inevitable headaches.

Financing The Dream

When we first began planning our around-the-world trip more than a decade ago, the financial aspect loomed large. Money is the main impediment that prevents most of us from pursuing anything—particularly of this magnitude. Travelling with a young family for seven months felt like a distant, almost impossible goal. But Janice and I were determined. We realized early on that achieving this dream wouldn't be about earning a windfall or making drastic changes overnight. Short of winning the lottery (which, I guess, is difficult to do when you don't play), we had a long road ahead to save for this trip.

> *Our strategy was about consistently making smart financial choices over the long term to ensure we could make this a reality.*

But it wasn't without doubts—especially when COVID-19 hit. Suddenly, the idea of taking a trip around the world felt like the most remote possibility in the midst of a global pandemic. The girls kept asking when things would go back to normal, and I had no answers for them. In those moments, I had serious doubts that this dream would ever materialize. It's human nature to assume that things will continue to go badly when you're in the thick of it, and, conversely, when times are good, it's hard to imagine they could take a turn for the worse. I was no exception. That uncertainty hung over us, but we kept moving forward as best as we could.

On top of the external uncertainties, there were moments when I questioned whether it was all worth it. What if something significant happened and all our work to save for the trip amounted to nothing? Are there better things we could do with the money instead? Have we saved enough money to begin with? These worst-case scenarios tend to run through your mind, and all you can do is cross your fingers and hope they stay hypothetical. You also start to wonder whether the short-term sacrifices—though I hesitate to call them that—are truly worth the long-term gain.

Looking back, I realize I could have enjoyed the process more. Involving the kids earlier, for instance, might have been a great opportunity to teach them about the importance of long-term planning.

To be honest, I worried they wouldn't keep the secret, but now I think it would have been a valuable lesson for them to see how hard we worked toward our financial goal each month, making progress little by little.

Through careful consideration and planning, we found ways to navigate our fears. Here are some of the strategies that allowed us to turn a decade of planning into a fully-funded, unforgettable experience.

1. No Car, No Problem

One of our most important financial decisions we made when we moved to Toronto was choosing to live without a car. While being within walking distance to transit made this manageable during pleasant weather, we faced our share of challenges—like shepherding kids to basketball practice in -20°C (-4°F) temperatures. Yet the financial benefits were substantial. Eliminating car payments, maintenance costs, insurance, and fuel translated into significant savings over the years. I've come to embrace this lifestyle, enjoying our neighbourhood walks, even though the kids initially protested. Now, they take unexpected transit delays or long walks in stride—it's simply our way of life. While friends outside the city often express disbelief at our car-free existence, questioning when we'll 'finally' get a vehicle, we've grown comfortable with our choice. Beyond the financial benefits, this lifestyle has exposed our children to Toronto's diverse reality through public transit. They've witnessed their city's social spectrum, from people struggling on the margins to suited professionals heading to Bay Street. Living car-free has challenged not only our habits but also societal norms, proving that alternative paths can be just as fulfilling, if not more so.

2. Minimal Extracurricular Activities

We chose a simpler approach to our kids' extracurricular activities, focusing on balance and affordability. Each year, both girls were enrolled in just one paid after-school activity. We carefully selected an activity to fit within our budget and, more importantly, within walking distance or close to transit. We did make an exception for Kasia to participate in ukulele lessons, as it was offered at school and the cost was minimal compared to some of the other activities we had come across. We were also fortunate to discover a fantastic local basketball program with a dedicated coach in a sport that, ironically, both Janice and I played when we were younger. This decision spared us the hassle of crisscrossing the city in the dead of winter for various activities. Instead, our weekends became a time to explore the city together, often finding free events or experiences to enjoy. It allowed us to embrace quality family time, unburdened by the usual stress of constant shuttling to and from different commitments.

3. Career Advancements in Toronto

Living and working in Toronto, the economic heart of Canada, opened up countless doors for career advancement. Both Janice and I were fortunate to find roles that not only aligned with our skills but also offered room for growth and new challenges. As we advanced in our careers, we were able to steadily increase our income, a benefit of living in a city with such a dynamic and diverse job market. Toronto's constant flow of opportunities in various industries allowed us to seize positions that elevated both our professional development and financial stability. This growth wasn't just about climbing the corporate ladder but about gaining the resources and flexibility to prioritize our long-term goals. The income we earned from these opportunities directly contributed to our ability to save faster, which ultimately made our dream of taking a trip around the world a reality.

4. The COVID-19 Effect

COVID-19 caught all of us off guard and played havoc with people's lives. We were fortunate to stay healthy during this period, and the virus significantly influenced our trip financial strategy. When the pandemic struck in March 2020, like many others, we transitioned to working from home and for the most part, continued to do so right up until our departure in early 2024. This change cut many of our daily expenses—work lunches disappeared, daycare was no longer necessary, and kids' activities came to a grinding halt. Socializing stopped, and life's typical spending patterns shifted. With stable incomes and a sharp reduction in our expenses, we were able to save more than we'd expected, and this unexpected surplus went straight to our travel fund. It was a bittersweet advantage for everyone during a difficult time globally, but it provided us with the extra push we needed.

5. Loyalty Points: The Hidden Treasure

We became avid collectors of loyalty points, especially through Air Canada's frequent flyer program, Aeroplan. This allowed us to focus on earning points and using their airline partners to travel the world. Over the years, Janice and I each signed up for credit cards that offered generous Aeroplan rewards, and as soon as each of our kids took their first flights at just three months old, we signed them up too. A major benefit we discovered later was the family sharing option via Aeroplan, which allowed us to pool our points. I have been fortunate to travel extensively over my career, collecting more points along the way, and this feature made it possible to combine all our points and use them for everyone's flights.

*Using points alone, our strategy helped us cover
about 75% of our family's airfare costs.*

My previous job, which involved a lot of international
travel, also added to our growing collection. I
accumulated more points than we ever expected by
consistently staying at the same hotel chain and flying
with the same airlines. One of the best perks was access
to airport lounges for our family of four throughout
our trip around the world. Not only did this make travel
more comfortable, but it also saved us a lot of money
on airport food. We no longer had to spend money
on overpriced snacks—fresh fruits, vegetables, and
whatever local delicacies were available in the lounge
were our go-tos. To this day, the kids still rave about the
food at Istanbul's international airport lounge!

One of the best decisions we made during the final
stages of planning was to book our flights and
accommodations as soon as the window opened. Most
airlines allow you to book flights 11 months, or 330
days, in advance, and as soon as we could, we started
locking things in. This gave us an advantage—whether it
was securing seats with points or having a wider variety
of Airbnb listings to choose from.

We also discovered that booking early meant we often required fewer points for our flights. The earlier we locked in our tickets, the fewer points were needed— especially for popular routes and times. Waiting until closer to departure often meant paying more points for the same seat. The same principle applied to Airbnb. In high-demand locations, we found that places were cheaper the further out we booked. When we later checked the same listings closer to our stay, they were significantly more expensive. Early preparation gave us the flexibility we needed and helped ensure that, after a decade of saving, our dream wouldn't be derailed by last-minute availability issues or rising prices.

6. Renting Out Our Home: A Lucky Break

One of the biggest financial wins came from an unexpected opportunity—we rented out our home. At first, we were reluctant to open our doors to someone we didn't know, especially while we'd be halfway around the world. We had never planned to rent it out, and the thought of a stranger in our home made us uneasy. But the universe, it seems, had other plans. We put up a For Lease sign, and a couple of days later, we found neighbours just a few houses down who needed a place to stay while their own home underwent major renovations. We had never met them before, but it felt like a perfect fit. In the end, it couldn't have worked out better. Having a trusted family so close to home gave us immense peace of mind, while also providing a steady source of income that helped cover the usual bills—mortgage, utilities, property taxes—and more, significantly offsetting our overall cost for the trip. What had started as a hesitant decision ended up being a financial relief and a key part of making our journey around the world possible.

Renting out our home also meant we had to declutter, and this turned out to be an unexpected but liberating experience. To prepare, we packed our winter clothes and personal essentials we didn't need for the trip into the smallest storage unit we could find. Everything else—excess items and knick-knacks—was either donated or discarded. Letting go of these unnecessary belongings created a lighter, simpler space, and it was a powerful reminder of how little we truly needed.

We left the house fully furnished for our tenants, but the decluttering process felt like a mini-move. It gave us the opportunity to evaluate every item we owned and decide whether it truly served a purpose. If it didn't, it was gone. In hindsight, this process perfectly reflected the theme of our trip: letting go of the old to make room for new experiences and a sense of freedom.

7. Cooking At Home More Often

Leading up to our trip, we committed to cooking at home more diligently to cut down on food expenses. This was an easy adjustment for us, as dining out had never been a frequent part of our routine. By preparing meals from scratch, we could control our budget, using versatile ingredients that stretched over multiple meals and avoiding the costs of restaurants. Batch cooking became a staple, with larger portions ensuring leftovers for the next day's meals, maximizing both our time and grocery budget. This habit not only saved us significant money but also instilled practical habits that we carried into our travels, making food planning smoother and more economical.

Additionally, we noticed another surprising source of savings: alcohol. During the year leading up to our trip, our alcohol consumption decreased considerably compared to during the pandemic period. The reduction in buying drinks—whether at home or out—added up quickly, creating a noticeable impact on our budget. These combined efforts of home-cooked meals and reduced spending on alcohol helped us build a more robust travel fund and reinforced mindful spending practices.

8. Finding Our Forever Home

When we purchased our home over a decade ago, we envisioned it as a starter home, with the option to upgrade to a larger house in the future as we built equity. While a larger, more modern space was appealing and something I knew we would all appreciate, we recognized that making this move would have delayed our plans by several years, turning our vision of travelling with pre-teens into an experience with teenagers—a different experience entirely. Instead, we chose to stay in our home, which had "good bones" and was in an exceptional neighbourhood with a warm, welcoming community. This decision allowed us to prioritize thoughtful renovations that made our home even more comfortable, without taking on significant new expenses. It also allowed us to focus our resources on saving for our sabbatical, placing value on meaningful experiences rather than expanding our living space. Ultimately, we embraced the idea that our home was already enough for our family, showing us that comfort and contentment could come from appreciating and enhancing what we already had.

9. Luck

Sometimes it feels uncomfortable to acknowledge how much luck plays a role in achieving big dreams.

So much of what we do is meticulously planned, carefully executed, and aimed at predictable results. We like to believe we are fully in control, masters of our destiny, shaping outcomes through sheer will and planning. Yet, we often conveniently forget those unforeseen factors—timely opportunities, chance encounters, and favourable circumstances—that influence our path and transform our carefully laid plans into reality. When I look back on the years leading up to our sabbatical, I can't deny the incredible amount of luck that helped pave the way.

One of the most serendipitous events was finding a young family on our very own street who needed a place to live precisely during the months we would be away. What were the chances of such perfect timing with neighbours so close by?

Then there was the unexpected benefit of my career. My last two jobs involved extensive international travel, taking me to Latin America, Israel, India, Japan, and beyond, allowing us to build Aeroplan miles and achieve higher preferred status—benefits that made our family trip more feasible and comfortable.

Even the timing of the pandemic played a surprising role. While COVID-19 brought unimaginable challenges and loss to so many, it also reshaped how schools adapted to remote learning. Because of this, we were able to keep up with our daughters' education through Google Classroom, a tool that had been barely used before but became standard post-pandemic. This digital access meant they didn't fall behind, despite the vast distances we travelled.

Perhaps most importantly, we stayed healthy throughout the trip, apart from some minor illnesses at the end. This meant no major disruptions that could have derailed our plans.

Reflecting on it all, I realize how luck intertwined with our diligent planning to make this trip a reality. We worked hard and made changes to our lifestyle, but I can't overlook the subtle yet profound role that good fortune played. Sometimes, the universe aligns in ways you can't foresee, turning dreams into lived experiences.

How Much Did it Cost?

Planning a seven-month trip around the world was an exercise in meticulous budgeting and financial preparation. Thanks to careful spending, we came in under budget, spending $115,000 CAD in total. Here's a breakdown of where the money went:

1. Flights and Transportation

- Total cost of flights: $25,000 CAD

  » Frequent flyer points covered approximately 75% of our flight costs, which greatly reduced our expenses and meant that we could have paid upwards of $100,000 CAD in total for flights.

2. Country-Specific Costs

Each country had its own budget, which included meals, accommodations, local transportation, activities, and miscellaneous expenses which totaled $88,000 CAD. Here's how it broke down per country:

Country	Duration (weeks)	Total Spent (CAD)
Australia	4	$16,000
New Zealand	4	$15,000
South Africa	4	$14,000
Thailand	3	$11,000
Jordan	2	$9,000
Albania	2	$8,000
The Philippines	3	$7,500
Ghana	2	$4,000
United Kingdom	<1	$3,500

The costs we incurred to maintain the house while we were away and expenses related to visas and vaccines were fully covered by the income we brought in from renting the house out.

Total Spending Overview

- Flights and Transportation: $25,000 CAD

- Country-Specific Costs: $88,000 CAD

Total Spending: $115,000 CAD

Looking back at our decade-long financial journey, what stands out isn't just the numbers, but the countless small decisions that made it possible. Living car-free, limiting activities while ensuring our kids still thrived, and advancing our careers in Toronto all contributed to our goal. Short of winning the lottery, we knew this dream required patience and persistence.

What's interesting about this endeavour is that most people focus on the end result—the grand adventure—but miss the thousand tiny decisions that built the bridge to get there. Our trip wasn't just seven months of memories; it was over a decade of choosing patience over instant gratification. We weren't perfect—heaven knows we had our share of missteps and second-guessing—but that's the thing about big dreams: they don't require perfection, just persistence.

Through strategic use of loyalty programs, unexpected COVID-19 savings, and rental income from our home, we turned what seemed financially impossible into reality. The total cost of $115,000 CAD might appear daunting, but broken down over years of intentional choices and careful planning, it became manageable. Our journey proves that with creativity and determination, the view from the mountaintop is worth every step of the climb.

Packing For An Extended Trip

Packing for such a long journey was a challenge in itself. We adhered to the well-known travel mantra: 'Take half the amount of stuff and twice the amount of money.' Simple in theory but requiring countless hours of scrutiny and resisting the temptation to overpack. Our goal was to pack only what we truly needed without being weighed down by excess luggage—a delicate balance when travelling for seven months with kids.

Adopting a 'less is more' philosophy throughout the packing process, we reviewed and revisited every single item before it made its way into our suitcases.

Each of us had just one carry-on suitcase and a backpack, which forced us to be strategic and thoughtful about every item we packed. We prioritized versatility, opting for clothing that could be layered, mixed, and matched. The key was to pack items that could serve multiple purposes with fewer pieces. This approach allowed us to travel light without feeling like we were missing anything essential.

A simple realization helped guide our packing choices: with rare exceptions, the basic necessities are available pretty much everywhere. We live in a globalized world, so whether we needed sunscreen in Amman, Jordan, or socks in Sarande, Albania, we knew we could find them along the way. This eased the pressure to pack for every possible scenario and kept our bags light.

One of the biggest factors that guided our packing choices was our deliberate decision to follow the sun. We planned our route to focus on warm-weather destinations, eliminating the need for bulky winter gear. This kept our luggage minimal and our travels more manageable. Avoiding heavy coats, boots, and extra layers gave us the freedom to pack light and stay nimble as we moved from place to place. After all, who wants to lug around winter coats and snow boots when you can pack shorts and flip-flops instead?

Another important consideration was that everything we brought needed to be easy to wash and quick to dry. We knew we'd be washing clothes frequently because of the warm weather, so we packed items made from fabrics that could handle regular wear and tear. By sticking to these basics, we simplified our packing process and kept our load light.

Each time, we asked ourselves, 'Do we really need this?' If the answer wasn't a resounding 'yes,' it stayed behind. This approach gave us the freedom to travel without the hassle of managing excessive luggage.

Choosing Destinations

Selecting our destinations was an adventure in itself, filled with a mix of strategic planning, geographic considerations, and a dash of wishful thinking. We stuck to the criteria of warm-weather destinations, places we hadn't been to, and what made sense geographically.

To be honest, by the time we were deep into planning, I was just ready to leave and see some sun. We could have gone anywhere, and I would have been happy. But, of course, we had to be a bit more thoughtful than that. Janice and I spent countless evenings with maps spread out on the kitchen table, debating the merits of various destinations.

We started with some hard truths: we wouldn't be able to travel to every continent, and we needed to prioritize. First on the list were places where we had family and friends we hadn't seen in a while—like Ghana, where my family is from; the Prairies in Canada, specifically Saskatchewan, to visit my in-laws and extended family, and London, UK, where my sibling lives. These locations were non-negotiable. Seeing familiar faces in far-off places was a comforting prospect for us and a way to share our adventure with those we loved.

Then came the dream destinations. Australia and New Zealand were at the top of the list. We'd always wanted to visit, and since they were so close to each other, it made sense to add both to the itinerary. We knew the kids would love the stunning landscapes, and it felt like the perfect opportunity to finally explore that part of the world. Thailand was also a clear choice, as we had first travelled there nearly 15 years ago before we had kids and wanted to rekindle that magic. The Philippines was more of an underdog, but we'd read so much about it being the best kept secret of Asia that we were eager to explore its charm. South Africa made the cut because we knew the kids would be thrilled to see the Lion King come to life in the wild as part of a safari.

Albania, too, piqued our interest in the most scientific way possible: we stared at a map of Europe, found it, looked up a few photos and videos, and thought, 'Well, that looks nice.' So we booked it.

With few people we knew having ever ventured to Albania, its status as an up-and-coming travel destination felt like an untapped treasure waiting to be discovered. The blend of its unique history and a reputation that promised adventure sealed the deal.

Jordan was the one destination that gave us pause. With the evolving situation in the Middle East, safety was a concern. But after careful research, we felt reassured it was safe, and the chance to float in the Dead Sea was an experience we didn't want to miss. We also decided to skip South America on this trip, having spent time there during our honeymoon and then again later with the kids.

Geographically, our route needed to make sense. We decided to travel westward from Toronto, leaving in January, moving steadily towards looping around the world and back again to ensure we'd arrive home back in time for another school year in September. This decision helped streamline our travel plans and reduced the likelihood of doubling back on ourselves.

To keep things exciting, we decided to keep the overall trip a secret from the kids. This meant that a lot of the decision-making was left to Janice and me, with many whispered conversations and hushed debates when the kids were either at school or fast asleep in bed. There were pros and cons to this approach. We wanted to see the excitement on their faces when we told them, but it also meant that they wouldn't get involved in the selection process of each country. We figured the happy medium was letting them choose activities in each country, giving them some control while keeping the destinations a surprise.

As departure day approached, the anticipation was almost unbearable. It was difficult to stay motivated at work or school as the weather grew colder and the days darker. We found ourselves scratching our heads, wondering why we hadn't planned to leave at the beginning of January, right after the holiday season, instead of later that month. The whole family was chomping at the bit to get out of town and soak up some sunshine.

In the end, our destinations were chosen with a mix of practicality and passion, ensuring a balance of familiar and new, economical and extravagant, always with an eye towards maximizing our experiences. We wanted this journey to be as enriching and enjoyable as possible, not just for Janice and me but for our kids as well. With our route mapped out and our bags almost packed, we were ready to embark on the adventure of a lifetime.

Finding Our Home Away From Home

Our research into accommodations was thorough and deliberate. We wanted each place we stayed to offer both comfort and a sense of local culture. After all, what's the point of travelling around the world if you end up in the same cookie-cutter hotel chains that could be anywhere? We aimed for a mix of unique local stays and occasional well-known hotels to keep things interesting and varied.

Staying in Airbnbs was our go-to strategy for a few reasons. They allowed us to have a home base in each location, which was crucial for maintaining a semblance of routine and stability, especially for the kids. We could cook our own meals, do laundry, and live more like locals than tourists. Additionally, being able to choose highly-rated places based on reviews gave us confidence in our decisions. Another significant advantage was that many Airbnbs offered ample space, providing us with room to move around and enjoy some quiet and solitude when we needed time away from each other. Sometimes, the biggest irritation with Airbnbs was the endless list of specific checkout demands that made us feel like we were preparing for a pop quiz. Some places required the garbage to be put in just the right spot, dishes washed, or sometimes, mysteriously, not washed but simply loaded into the dishwasher. Fine, no problem, except—plot twist—there was a cleaning fee. We did most of the cleaning ourselves—but I guess we were just paying for the privilege to do the initial clean for them.

We didn't want to completely forgo the conveniences and amenities of well-known hotels. Sometimes, you just need a complimentary buffet breakfast and a swimming pool to unwind. These stays provided a nice break from the unpredictability of other accommodations and were especially appreciated after long flights or car rides. They also offered opportunities to interact with other travellers and get recommendations from concierges familiar with the area, which often revealed a diamond in the rough that you wouldn't find online.

Overall, our approach to accommodations balanced comfort, convenience, cost, and cultural immersion. We wanted our kids to experience the world in a way that was engaging and educational, yet enjoyable. By mixing local stays with traditional hotels, we created a diverse and enriching travel experience that met all our needs.

Learning On The Go

To make their studies seamless we took their teachers' advice and focused on the basics—reading, writing, and arithmetic—in French, since the girls were in French Immersion, which added a whole new level of complexity. The memories of pandemic homeschooling still haunted me like a bad dream, but this time, we had a more creative approach to keep things fun and manageable. I'd like to say it involved more educational adventures, but honestly, sometimes it was mostly me googling 'How to teach fractions in French while in Thailand.'

Before we departed, their teachers were incredibly supportive, providing us with guidance on what to focus on and, most importantly, encouraging us to enjoy the experience. This support was invaluable, as it gave us a clear framework and the confidence to integrate learning into our daily travels. The girls enjoyed posting pictures of the trip on their Google Classroom platform.

We tried to embed education seamlessly into our journey. For reading, we leveraged the Libby app, which enabled us to borrow books virtually from our local library in Toronto to read during travels. The girls, already with a keen eye for reading, turned into avid readers with a thirst for knowledge about what they experienced or desire to research where we would visit next.

For writing, they kept journals, documenting their experiences, which not only improved their writing skills but also helped them reflect on their adventures. Their grandma, a former educator, helped out significantly by creating an invaluable travel book for each of the girls. This book required them to remember and synthesize key points from each place we visited. They noted what they saw, the type of currency used, and details about the local food and political structure. This book became a treasure trove of memories and learning, and it was a fantastic way for them to engage and remember their experiences.

Arithmetic lessons took on a whole new level of importance during our travels, as the girls quickly became proficient in managing their souvenir money and budgeting for their favourite street foods. They learned to calculate, convert currencies, and even keep track of getting the correct change.

But one of the interesting lessons came when they realized they could loan us money. Their aunty had generously given each of them the equivalent of $20 Canadian dollars in every country we visited as a Christmas gift, which turned out to be a lifesaver— not just for them but for Janice and me as well. When a store didn't accept credit cards and Mom and Dad were short on cash, our girls were more than happy to 'lend' us some of theirs—with interest, of course. Ayana, in particular, was quick to remind us that she wasn't running a charity. It wasn't long before Kasia followed suit, turning our small debts into what felt like complex loan agreements. They were suddenly little bankers, reminding us that the interest rate increased daily if we didn't pay them back quickly enough.

Language immersion was another key component. Whenever we heard French-speaking tourists around us, we encouraged the kids to practice their French. This real-world practice was invaluable, as it continued to boost their confidence and fluency in the language.

Museums and cultural experiences became a core part of their curriculum. For example, visiting the Te Papa Museum in Wellington, New Zealand was an exceptional experience for the girls to learn more about the indigenous Maori culture. I can remember the girls' heads spinning in wonder when they learned that elephants can sleep while standing up or leaning against a tree for support while on safari in South Africa.

One of the most rewarding aspects of our journey was hearing the kids talk to their friends about our travels, especially when they missed home. Despite often rolling their eyes when I tried to emphasize the lessons we were learning along the way, it was amazing to see the level of detail they remembered and shared with their friends. They would relay stories with such enthusiasm, describing their experiences with passion and focus. It was fascinating to see what they highlighted, like the idiosyncrasies of the animals on safari or their unexpected fascination with Bedouin chess in Jordan, something they had initially feigned interest in. While my attempts to tie lessons to our travels might not yield real-time results, I've learned that our little sponges soak up more than we give them credit for. What I quickly learned was that, if they can't discuss it with you immediately, fear not—they're just saving the conversation for a moment when it's most inconvenient for you.

Though I often thought certain things might go unnoticed or seem unimportant to them, their perspectives were different from ours. What I might have glossed over, like small cultural moments or intricate details of our surroundings, became significant learning points for them. Watching them eagerly share their newfound knowledge showed me just how much they were absorbing, even when they were completely tuning me out at the time.

Integrating education into our travel routine required a lot of planning and effort, but it was immensely rewarding. The kids not only kept up with their schoolwork but also gained a wealth of knowledge and experiences that no traditional classroom could offer. This hands-on learning approach enriched their education and made our journey even more meaningful.

Leaving Our Jobs: A Leap of Faith

Deciding to leave our jobs for seven months was one of the toughest aspects of planning our journey. Both Janice and I had roles we enjoyed and were passionate about. In Western culture, much of our identity is often tied to what we do for a living—it's like a badge of honour we wear, a tangible way to show that we are contributing members of society. Our careers gave us that validation, a sense of purpose and worth that went beyond just providing for our family. Walking away from that, even temporarily, felt like losing a part of who we were.

It wasn't just about leaving behind the day-to-day grind or wondering how our employers would react— it was about the unsettling thought of stepping away from something that had defined us for so long. What happens when that part of your identity is gone and you no longer have that external validation? It's easy to wear your career as a mark of success, but taking the leap to leave behind those steady roles—even for something as incredible as a round-the-world trip—felt like a tough pill to swallow. While the challenge of letting go was real, it was temporary, and we found ourselves questioning it mostly before the trip and during the first few weeks after leaving Canada. Over time, the uncertainty faded, replaced by a growing sense of freedom and adventure.

Approaching our employers felt like preparing for battle—we rehearsed our conversations over and over, worried about how they would take the news. Would they understand? Fortunately, they were incredibly supportive, recognizing the value of the experience we were about to embark on. Still, even with their backing, the gnawing feeling remained—what if the roles we loved weren't there when we came back? What if the professional landscape changed during our seven-month absence, making it a bit harder to pick up where we left off?

These were the fears we wrestled with, but we also recognized that this was a once-in-a-lifetime opportunity, something we couldn't pass up. Our confidence came from the unique careers we had built—both Janice and I knew that the skills and experience we'd gained over the years would serve us well, no matter what awaited us on our return. And while it was unnerving to leave behind such a central part of our identities, we believed that new doors would open when the time came.

For us, it wasn't just about stepping away from our jobs temporarily—it was about questioning everything we'd been taught about success, security, and what makes a life 'well-lived.' Sure, we had spreadsheets full of numbers and plans, but what we really needed was the courage to believe that life wouldn't fall apart if we stepped away from the script we'd been following. That maybe, just maybe, our worth wasn't tied to our job titles or our LinkedIn profiles. Looking back now, I realize that sometimes the biggest risk isn't taking the leap—it's staying put and wondering 'what if?' for the rest of your life. Because here's the thing about comfort zones: they're great places to visit, but dangerous places to stay too long.

Key Takeaways

1. Less is More: Emphasizing the importance of packing light by prioritizing versatile items and recognizing the availability of essentials globally can lead to a more enjoyable and manageable journey.

2. Travel as a Powerful Learning Tool: Integrating real-world experiences into children's education can foster curiosity and critical thinking, demonstrating that travel provides unique opportunities for growth beyond the classroom.

3. Sustaining Dreams Through Patience and Vision: Achieving a dream, no matter how big, requires not just effort but the ability to sustain that effort over time, proving that deliberate choices made over years can lead to remarkable, life-changing results.

Key Questions

1. How do you balance the excitement of spontaneous adventures with the need for careful planning when travelling?

2. What are the most significant life lessons you've learned from travelling, and how do they inform your values and decisions at home?

3. How has your perspective on travel changed over time, and what experiences have influenced this evolution?

PAUSE & REFLECT: Building Your Foundation

1. Create Your Roadmap

   TODAY: Write down your top 3 life goals and one small step you can take toward each

   THIS WEEK: Create a vision board or detailed plan for your most important goal

   THIS MONTH: Research and map out the financial requirements for your primary goal — whether it's travel, starting a business, buying a home, or pursuing further education

2. Practice Minimalism

   - Evaluate your commitments and learn to say "no" to what doesn't align with your goals

   - Create systems for maintaining organization in key areas (physical spaces, digital files, time management)

   - Practice mindful consumption—be intentional about what you allow into your life

3. Build Support Systems

   - Share your dreams with one trusted friend or family member who can offer honest feedback

   - Identify three mentors in different areas of your life (personal, professional, financial)

   - Create a "skills exchange" list—what you can offer others and what you need help with

CHAPTER #3
THAILAND

"Travel isn't always comfortable.
But discomfort is the price you pay for a great story."
- Paul Theroux

Thailand is a tourism powerhouse. Every facet of the country is geared toward ensuring it continues to generate foreign investment from tourism. For Janice and me, our second visit brought back memories from nearly 15 years ago when we first visited the country. This time, however, the experience was vastly different, primarily because we had two kids in tow.

The sheer number of farang (foreigners in Thai) pouring into Thailand each year is mind-blowing. Last year, Thailand threw open its doors to a whopping 40 million tourists. Imagine if every single Canadian decided to pack up and say, 'Forget the snow, let's head to Thailand!' In fact, tourism makes up 15% of the country's GDP, so they've definitely perfected the art of the tourist experience. In Bangkok, everywhere you turn, it's a steady stream of offers and questions. At first, it's funny, but after a few hours in the blazing 40°C (100°F) heat, it feels like you're in a live comedy sketch where every punchline is, 'No, I don't need a pet elephant named Bob,' 'No, I'm not in the market for coconut bras,' and my personal favourite, 'No, I really don't need a selfie stick that doubles as a back scratcher.' The moment you step outside your hotel, it's like everyone's auditioning for the role of your personal guide with a cheery 'Where you going?' And no matter what you say, it's never the answer they're looking for. So you just nod, smile, and hope they won't follow you too far down the street.

The night markets are a spectacle to behold. With street performers pulling off dance moves that would leave Beyoncé speechless, quirky arts and crafts that would put your grandma's kitschy decor to shame, and food stalls serving up an endless feast, it was a non-stop adventure. We saw everything from squirming larvae to glossy black scorpions, which, believe it or not, are considered local delicacies. But the showstopper for the most jaw-dropping dish has to be... drumroll... crocodile tongue!

Yep, you read that right.

It's supposedly packed with protein and every essential amino acid. Then again, so are beef, chicken, fish, and eggs.... Ayana, bless her, had a moment of pure concern over a barbecued duck hanging in one stall. "What animal is that?" she asked, wide-eyed. I explained, "It's a duck," to which she replied, "Well, it looks kind of sad." "Probably because it's, you know... dead," I told her.

We wanted to immerse ourselves in Thai culture, so we signed up for what was advertised as an 'innocuous' Muay Thai Family session. Muay Thai, a martial art developed in Thailand, allows strikes with fists, elbows, knees, and shins.

Innocuous? Not so much.

The kids thought it would be like a fun jungle gym experience, while I expected a family bonding afternoon with a little bit of exercise. However, as soon as we arrived, we were greeted by the sight of skilled Muay Thai fighters undergoing intense training sessions. I immediately thought to myself, 'Thank goodness our session won't turn out to be like that.'

Famous last words.

Even though I tried to keep up with my own workouts during our travels, I quickly realized I was nowhere near prepared for what lay ahead. After introducing ourselves, we were promptly instructed (or more accurately, demanded) to warm up by skipping rope for 15 minutes. Now, I can't recall the last time I skipped rope, but I do remember thinking it would be an easy warm-up. Two minutes in, I was already exhausted. However, I wasn't about to show it—I didn't want to disappoint the trainer, and more importantly, I didn't want to disappoint myself.

The trainer then led us through a series of drills designed to get us 'fight ready.' I have always been a sweating machine, but this experience was something else. I was sweating so much that I couldn't tell whether I was slipping on my own sweat or the water I was drinking. I felt like I was drowning in perspiration. To my amusement (and a bit of relief), the instructor was even harder on the girls. Ayana shot me a pleading look when the instructor insisted she do sit-ups. She looked at me as if to say, 'Do I really have to listen to this crazy man?' I wasn't about to intervene—if I did, I was worried he might make me join her.

At another point, Kasia whispered to me between push-ups, "Daddy, are you sure he doesn't think I'm a professional Muay Thai boxer?" Smiling through the pain, I assured her, "No, honey. I think he just wants to see what we're made of." She quipped, "Well, Daddy, it looks like you're made of sweat."

There we were, paying good money to be tortured. Lesson learned: when a Muay Thai class is advertised as 'suitable for families,' just go get a massage instead.

Thinking back, we have had plenty of memorable moments in Thailand, and not all of them were planned. One such adventure occurred during a day trip to the islands off the coast of Koh Lanta, an island paradise in the middle of the Pacific. We rose early, hired a boat, and set out to explore neighbouring islands, swimming in the sea and soaking in the stunning scenery.

As we meandered through a maze of mangroves, our boat captain casually asked if we were interested in seeing some of the island's monkeys. Janice, still traumatized from a past encounter with monkeys in Indonesia, was hesitant. But I confidently reassured her, "It'll be fine."

The captain steered the boat closer to the shore, and we saw the monkeys perched in the trees. The girls oohed and aahed, snapping a few photos. We were content, but the captain had other plans. He decided to take a cigarette break and, in the process, began throwing food at the monkeys. I knew this was a bad idea.

Rule number one: Never feed wild animals.

But he was the captain, and, of course, I told myself, he had done this a million times, so I trusted him.

As the boat drifted closer, Ayana innocently asked, "Can monkeys swim?" Janice and I exchanged glances. Based on our (limited) knowledge of monkeys, we assumed they couldn't. I shook my head no—about to give her a long explanation when she interrupted me and pointed, "Then why is that monkey swimming towards us?"

Our hearts sank. Apparently, monkeys can swim, and quite well, too. In no time, the little guy was aboard our boat, rummaging for food.

Chaos ensued.

We fled to the other side of the boat while the captain and his assistant tried to shoo the monkey away, offering it more food in a desperate attempt to satisfy its appetite. But this monkey was no amateur—it wanted more than the captain's offerings. With shocking dexterity, it opened a water bottle, chugged it, and then hurled the empty bottle at the kids.

They screamed.

And just when we thought it couldn't get any wilder, the monkey took hold of the steering wheel, trying to steer the boat as if it had some grand destination in mind. It was not exactly the peaceful boat ride we had envisioned.

As the monkey raced around the boat searching for more treats, I couldn't help but wonder whether all the food the captain was tossing was our lunch for the day. If so, I thought, let the monkey have it. I immediately dismissed the thoughts in my head from all the movies I watched about negotiating with terrorists. This was going to be an exception.

Finally, after what felt like hours (but was probably only minutes), the monkey had its fill—or perhaps grew tired of our lackluster provisions—and leaped back into the water, swimming away as nonchalantly as it had arrived. We sped off to our next destination, too shocked to speak. Our monkey encounter left us in stunned silence, but eventually, Janice just burst into laughter, and the rest of us couldn't help but chuckle at what had just happened. It's these unexpected moments that make us shake our heads and wonder what we had truly got out ourselves into.

In northern Thailand, Chiang Mai is home to numerous elephant sanctuaries, many of which have shifted their focus from elephant rides and performances to more ethical experiences, like walking alongside elephants in the wild. We spent a day at one of these sanctuaries, watching these magnificent creatures roam freely.

Then, we discovered a unique activity: making paper and creative arts and crafts from elephant poo.

Yes, you read that correctly.

Naturally, I was skeptical. I asked Janice, "Do we really want to do this? Won't it smell awful?" But she encouraged me to keep an open mind, and the kids, of course, were all in.

Surprisingly, there was no smell at all. It turns out that because elephants are herbivores, their droppings don't contain the same odour-causing compounds found in the poo of human beings, even those that are vegetarian or even vegan. We were guided through the entire process, which involved cleaning the poo, breaking it down into fibres, and eventually transforming it into paper. The process was fascinating, and the kids were hands-on, shaping the fibres into sheets of paper to dry in the sun.

Afterward, we even had the chance to create arts and crafts using our freshly made paper. I had to admire their business model: we paid to enter the facility, go on a 'tour' to make elephant poo paper, and then paid again to buy the crafts we made. Who needs employees when your customers are willing to do the work for you for free?

While that was a fun, hands-on activity, Thailand offered me a different kind of hands-on experience in Chiang Mai—this time, quite literally. Janice had discovered a massage clinic unlike any other, where ex-convicts were employed as massage therapists. The idea intrigued me, so I decided to check it out early the next day, without the kids.

As I waited, a large, armoured truck pulled up. To my surprise, the 'massage therapists' exited the truck one by one in handcuffs. I was confused—weren't these supposed to be ex-convicts? I asked the man next to me, who casually informed me that, no, these were actual convicts still serving time. Before I could process that fully, a receptionist beckoned me over and asked what kind of treatment I wanted. Noticing my hesitation, she smiled and reassured me, "Don't worry, only a few of them killed their husbands." She winked. I thought to myself, 'Well, you only live once...' though I made a mental note to remind Janice of my location, just in case this turned into my last adventure.

As I lay down, I kept thinking, was she the one who killed her husband or was it the other massage therapist beside me whose client was screaming in agony during his massage? It took me a good while to relax, and she could sense that and told me to take a few deep breaths. To my surprise, the experience was incredible. My therapist, Mae, was gentle yet firm, her hands working out knots I didn't even know existed. As I drifted into a state of relaxation, the irony of the situation wasn't lost on me. I fell asleep, and she gently woke me up to flip me over. She was very good. I had relaxed and was feeling calm and serene. I thanked her profusely and promised to return. Because why wouldn't I? I survived, didn't I? All I knew was that this was one of the best Thai massages ever.

The way our mind works is funny isn't it? We walk around with these neat little boxes where we file people away - 'safe,' 'dangerous,' 'trustworthy,' 'stay away.' But life has this way of messing with those boxes, of showing us how paper-thin our assumptions really are. And while my brain was spinning worst-case scenarios (thanks, overactive imagination), my intuition was picking up on something else: the genuine care in the staff's demeanor, the professional setup, the government oversight.

Truth is, I tend to dive into these kinds of situations more often than most — whether it's impromptu trips to remote villages, accepting dinner invitations from locals, or, yes, getting massages from current inmates. There's a sweet spot between being so guarded that we miss out on extraordinary experiences and being so open that we ignore red flags. It's not necessarily about throwing caution to the wind; it's about learning to figure out which way the wind is trying to guide you. I guess—like most people—I am still trying to figure it out.

We continued to immerse ourselves in the unique culture of Chiang Mai, discovering experiences that stretched our minds and tested our patience in unexpected ways. One particularly memorable moment was participating in a 'monk chat,' where we sat down with Buddhist monks to gain insight into their path to enlightenment and their perspective on life. The girls, with their unfiltered curiosity, asked a range of questions—from deep philosophical queries about happiness to practical dilemmas, like how to handle frequent sibling arguments.

Our monk shared a simple yet profound approach: to pause and breathe deeply when conflicts arise, and to focus on listening to each other's feelings before responding. He likened it to tying a knot—pulling too hard only makes it tighter, but slowing down and loosening the tension helps untangle it.

The monk's advice was put to the test when the girls started squabbling over who got the bigger pancake at breakfast the next morning. I tried to remind them of the monk's tying a knot analogy, but my attempt at calm was met by Kasia with a pointed response, "Maybe the monk doesn't understand pancakes."

Clearly, enlightenment has its limits.

Key Takeaways

1. Embrace Discomfort: Pushing through challenging experiences can strengthen family bonds and create memorable stories.

2. Practice Compassion: Understanding the stories behind people fosters empathy and personal growth.

3. Find Humour in Challenges: Laughter can transform awkward situations into long lasting memories.

Key Questions

1. What are some of the most memorable or humorous moments you've experienced while travelling? How did these moments shape your overall view of the trip?

2. What unique cultural practices have I encountered, and how have they impacted my perspective?

3. In what ways can I seek out authentic experiences in my travels or daily life?

PAUSE & REFLECT: Embracing Challenge

1. Cultivate Mindful Moments

    TODAY: Notice three instances where you rush through an experience, then try the same activity again but slower

    THIS WEEK: Practice the monk's "loosening the knot" technique when facing a frustrating situation

    THIS MONTH: Create designated "no-agenda" times in your schedule where you let experiences unfold naturally

2. Challenge Comfort Zones

    •   Sign up for a fitness class that intimidates you - whether it's kickboxing, hot yoga, or dance

    •   Take a lesson in something completely foreign to you, like playing a traditional instrument or learning calligraphy

    •   Join a local group where you'll be the obvious new-comer or minority, embracing the discomfort of being different

3. Embrace Spontaneity

    •   Strike up a conversation with someone whose life seems very different from yours

    •   Say yes to an invitation or opportunity that you'd normally decline out of uncertainty

    •   Put yourself in an unfamiliar environment - whether it's a new neighborhood, cultural center, or commu-nity gathering - and stay there long enough to feel comfortable

A crunchy new take on
protein—would you try it?

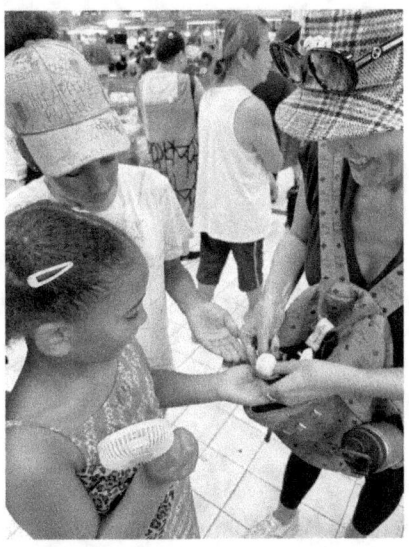

A little sweat, a lot of taste—
worth every bite.

A swing with a view.

A temple through two lenses,
each telling its own story.

Adding a little bite to your meal.

Dipping into new flavors and loving every bite.

From blank shirts to family masterpieces.

Lunch is served!

In awe of these gentle giants, roaming free.

Little chef in the making!

Ayana's got the chops!

Lost in the endless horizon.

Partners in crime, making a big splash.

Taking in the world, one tuk-tuk ride at a time.

When adventure really stinks.

CHAPTER #4
AUSTRALIA

"The only impossible journey is the one you never begin."
– Tony Robbins

Our Australian adventure kicked off with a moment that could only be described as 'driver's ed meets reality TV'—learning to drive on the left-hand side of the road. I had been dreading it for weeks. Remembering to drive on the right—or rather, the left—felt like one of the more daunting challenges of our trip. I slipped behind the wheel of our rental car, gripping it as if it were my lifeline. Slowly, I eased the car out of the parking lot, trying to commit to memory all the new rules while avoiding any very expensive mistakes. Then came the unsolicited encouragement from the backseat: "Way to go, Daddy! You moved the car a whole inch—gold star!" Ayana's enthusiasm, as always, was… sarcastically overwhelming. But, if driving on the opposite side of the road was our first challenge, Australia had a few more curveballs in store. Each one, however, came with a reward that turned out to be far more enriching than we'd imagined.

One of the first things we had to adapt to in tropical Australia was the infamous 'stinger season.' Lasting from October to May, this dangerous period occurs because the warm, calm waters of the tropical regions are ideal for marine stingers to reproduce and travel down the coastline. It was a reality we hadn't fully understood until we arrived just north of Airlie Beach. The beaches—pristine, with stretches of golden sand and crystal-clear waters—looked like something straight out of a postcard, yet they were mostly off-limits, thanks to deadly jellyfish. Box jellyfish and the elusive Irukandji, the size of an adult fingernail, could turn a dream day at the beach into a nightmare. The vinegar stations, which dotted the coastline, were a reminder of the lurking danger. Vinegar, as we quickly learned, is the first line of defence for anyone unfortunate enough to get stung, helping to neutralize the venom until medical help could arrive.

It was unsettling to realize just how dangerous the ocean could be in such a beautiful setting. We found ourselves walking along the beach, appreciating the view from a safe distance. In some places, large stinger nets were set up to keep jellyfish out, creating 'safe' swimming zones. However, the sight of these nets didn't exactly calm the girls' nerves. Ok, ok more me than them. The idea of swimming in a netted-off section didn't sit well with us, so we opted for the numerous public pools scattered along the coast. These pools, family-friendly and free of charge, were an absolute godsend, providing the perfect alternative to the risky beach waters. Soon, our daily ritual revolved around jumping into the cool, clear waters of these pools, and the allure of the beach faded into the background as we created our own fun.

But Australia's wildlife had plenty of surprises for us. The white ibis, often referred to as the 'bin chicken,' quickly became our uninvited mascot. These birds, relentless in their pursuit of food, are notorious for rummaging through trash. They reminded me of raccoons back home in Canada—determined, sneaky, and always looking for an easy meal. Our first encounter with a bin chicken was sooner than we expected. We were sitting at a laid-back, sun-soaked beachside café when we witnessed the remarkable antics of one particularly brazen ibis. As a woman nearby savoured her lunch, a hungry ibis swooped in with astonishing precision, snatching a French fry from her fingers before anyone could react. The woman was stunned for a second, and we could do nothing but watch in amusement.

It was at that moment that we truly understood the purpose of the water spray bottles sitting at every table. They weren't for cooling off in the Aussie heat; they were makeshift defences against these relentless bird bandits. Diners were armed and ready, spritzing any ibis that dared to get too close, but it was clear: these birds had mastered the art of snatch-and-dash. Even armed with spray bottles, we watched as the ibis continued its antics, reminding us that sometimes, even wildlife thrives on a good laugh.

One of the highlights for all of us in Australia was the mystical wonders of the Daintree Forest. The Daintree Rainforest is Australia's largest tropical rainforest, home to ancient ecosystems and unique wildlife. Here, our indigenous tour guide, Skip, became our gatekeeper to the secrets of the world's oldest rainforest, where the majority of Australia's wildlife finds its home. You could tell Skip was having way too much fun showing us the forest's greatest hits of deadly creatures — especially when he got to the world's most lethal plant and a spider that could make your last moments really, really uncomfortable.

As Skip led us deeper into the rainforest, cheerfully listing off deadly plant after deadly animal, our group got quieter and quieter—funny how knowing everything around you could kill you tends to do that.

The other family on our tour wasn't handling it well—their kids were in tears, and honestly, I was close behind. While I was having my own internal meltdown about whether this whole rainforest thing was genius or just plain bad idea, one of their girls wailed, 'I'm too young to die!' The dad in me couldn't help but quip, 'Hey, if you make it out of here alive you will have a great story for show-and-tell!' Pretty sure that didn't exactly reassure anyone.

Thank goodness Skip read the room—he switched gears from death and doom to showing us something pretty cool. Suddenly we were all scrubbing sarsaparilla leaves to make soap and learning how to turn stems into nature's Vicks VapoRub. The girls loved it, and honestly, who knew the rainforest was basically a natural pharmacy?

After surviving Skip's tour of deadly creatures, we were ready for some less adventurous Australian experiences—though even ordering dinner would require adapting to new customs.

Dining in Australia took a little getting used to. Unlike in North America, where tipping is the norm and waitstaff are constantly hovering, Australia's approach is far more relaxed. At pubs and casual eateries, you order at the bar, grab your order number, and find a seat. The staff will eventually bring your food to you. But tipping—not a thing. At first, we kept calculating the tip in our heads when we paid, but then we realized—service staff in Australia earn a living wage, so there's no expectation to tip. It was a refreshing change after the tipping culture we were used to, where it felt like you were supposed to tip for just about everything.

This self-service approach, while practical, led to some humorous moments. I remember one evening at a pub, where we spent a good 15 minutes chatting, only to realize no one had come to take our order because, well, we were supposed to go up to the bar ourselves. It was a funny reminder of how different customs can be, even for something as simple as ordering dinner.

Australia's laid-back lifestyle was something you couldn't help but absorb. There was no rush—no sense of urgency to anything. People took their time, and life outdoors seemed to be at the very heart of it all. Everywhere you looked, there was a deep connection to nature. Whether it was a surf session after work, a swim at the beach, or a drink at the pub, it was clear that outdoor living wasn't just a pastime—it was a way of life. We quickly came to appreciate this balance between work and play, where time spent outdoors was just as important as anything else.

Alexandra Promenade is a beautiful and busy street that runs parallel to the Pacific Ocean in the seaside resort of Maroochydore (pronounced Mah-roo-chee-door). Every morning the migration of what seems like the world's fittest people descends upon the rough seas. The masses are early to rise, surf, sunbathe, and swim— it's like a daily movie shoot, and I feel like an extra.

During one of my walks, I was doling out my "Mornings!" or "G'day Mate!" to whomever caught my eye as I walked along the promenade. An elderly gentleman, oblivious to my presence, decides the street is his changing room. With the determination of a man on a mission (or perhaps just an aversion to walking a few hundred meters to the change room), he stripped down naked right then and there.

As fate would have it, my footsteps startled him mid-change, and without missing a beat, he turned to me in his full birthday suit and cheerfully exclaimed, "G'day Mate!" If there were ever a masterclass in confidence, this was it.

You know what's funny about life? Sometimes our biggest lessons come from the most ridiculous moments. While most of us are out there overthinking every little thing— worried about how we look, what people think, if our hair's doing that weird thing again—I haven't had that feeling in a long time—this guy had it all figured out. Stark naked on a public street, and instead of panicking or diving behind a bush, he just throws out a casual 'G'day Mate!' like he's fully dressed at a coffee shop. Talk about owning the moment. Maybe that's what real confidence looks like—not the polished, Instagram-worthy kind, but the ability to be caught completely exposed and still act like it's just another Tuesday morning.

Living near the beach in Maroochydore took a bit of getting used to. On a trip to the grocery store, I was struck by how casual the dress code was—shirts were optional, flip-flops were a must, and towels seemed to be the latest fashion trend. I kept doing double takes, watching people walk down aisles with towels slung around their necks, juggling grocery baskets, while I clutched my t-shirt like it was the last thing standing between me and full-blown embarrassment. Every aisle felt like a fashion runway, and, clearly, I wasn't on the guest list.

We quickly grew fond of the public spaces throughout Australia—clean restrooms, outdoor BBQs, well-maintained playgrounds—it was all part of the lifestyle. Whether it was having a meal under the sun or watching the kids play, it was impossible not to feel more connected to nature. You almost became 'outdoorsy' by osmosis.

One of the most surreal experiences we had was kayaking in the Pacific Ocean with dolphins. The moment was almost too perfect to believe. Janice and

Kasia were in one kayak, Ayana and I in another. The waves were higher than I'd anticipated, and each stroke felt like a battle against the water. I worried that our kayak would flip at any moment, but Ayana's determination kept us going. Her confidence in the water was contagious, and together, we pushed through the choppy waves until we reached the calm. That's when the dolphins appeared, swimming gracefully alongside us, playful and completely unbothered by our presence. I watched Ayana's face light up as she saw them, her joy reflecting my own. It was one of those rare, perfect moments that I'll carry with me forever.

When I reflect on that experience, it taught me that sometimes you have to paddle through the rough stuff to get to the good stuff. There we were, arms burning, waves tossing us around like we were nothing, and I'm sitting there thinking 'What did I get us into?' But that's the thing about pushing past your comfort zone—just when you're ready to call it quits, when you're questioning all your life choices, that's when life throws you something magical. Those dolphins didn't show up during the easy part. Nope, they waited until we'd fought our way through the choppy waters, until we'd proven to ourselves that we could handle more than we thought. Kind of makes you wonder how many amazing moments we miss out on just because we turn back when things get tough. Sometimes the universe saves its best surprises for the other side of 'I can't do this.'

Despite Australia's reputation for dangerous wildlife, we quickly learned that the actual threats were less terrifying than the stories made them out to be. Sure, there were venomous creatures, but most of our encounters with wildlife were serene rather than spine-chilling. The real challenge came in adjusting to the quirks of Australian life, especially what we affectionately called the 'Sydney Shuffle.' After years of navigating the world on the right side, old habits die hard. Every day felt like an opportunity to showcase my awkward dance moves as I tried to adapt to the left. Whether dodging pedestrians on the sidewalk or trying to figure out which lane to drive in, we were kept on our toes. But, as with everything in life, this learning curve was exactly what we needed.

Australia pushed us out of our comfort zones in ways we hadn't anticipated. From navigating new driving rules to sidestepping bin chickens and jellyfish, each experience taught us to adapt and embrace the unexpected. By the end of our time there, we found ourselves not just surviving but thriving in a world that felt both familiar and wildly different. The lesson? Growth happens in the moments when you're willing to take a detour and discover new rhythms of life.

Key Takeaways

1. Finding Freedom in Exposure: Adventures often require us to be exposed—not just physically but emotionally. Embracing this vulnerability can lead to greater self-acceptance and a richer understanding of our place in the world.

2. Adventure as a Catalyst for Self-Discovery: Engaging in new experiences can lead to profound insights about ourselves, revealing strengths and passions that may have remained hidden in familiar settings.

3. Resilience Through Experience: Facing and overcoming obstacles during our adventures builds resilience, teaching us that discomfort can often be a precursor to personal growth and deeper connections with others.

Key Questions

1. How do we define adventure in our lives, and what does stepping out of our comfort zones reveal about our true selves?

2. What lessons can we learn from the rawness and innocence of being exposed, both literally and figuratively, in a world that often encourages us to hide behind facades?

PAUSE & REFLECT: Embracing New Perspectives

1. Embrace Exposure

   TODAY: Choose authenticity over appearances in one situation - speak your truth in a meeting, wear what feels comfortable, or admit when you don't know something.

   THIS WEEK: Practice being comfortable in your own skin - try an activity you've avoided due to self-consciousness, dine alone, or share a story you usually keep private.

   THIS MONTH: Let go of one social expectation that holds you back - whether it's maintaining a certain image or conforming to others' ideas of success. Notice how this freedom changes your daily experience.

2. Live Unmasked

   • Leave your perfectly curated self at home for a day.

   • Take up space without apologizing.

   • Toast to imperfect moments, like getting caught in your birthday suit!

3. Quiet Confidence

   • Find strength in stillness instead of constant motion.

   • Release the need to explain your choices.

A bite of reality - better to have it and not need it!

Checking out the views of Blue Mountain.

Cooling off with the kids in Cairns.

Defending our fries: the great bin chicken showdown!

Finding Nemo and friends in their natural habitat.

Hands on learning - turning leaves into lather.

Looking for dolphins in the Pacific.

When in doubt, improvise -playing basketball with a soccer ball.

Seas the moment - a little pail, endless horizons.

Chasing the light at the end of the tunnel.

CHAPTER #5
THE PHILIPPINES

"Judge a society by how it treats strangers, not friends."
- Malcolm Gladwell

From the moment we arrived, it became clear that the Philippines' greatest treasure wasn't its stunning beaches or awe-inspiring landscapes—it was its people.

Smiling faces, calm demeanors, and a readiness for casual chit-chat met us at every turn. If there was a place where friendliness could be measured, this country would set the gold standard.

However, our landing set the tone and it was a bit more eventful than I had anticipated.

Sometimes, a journey begins with a jolt, a reminder that adventure doesn't wait for you to feel ready. Our landing in the Philippines set the tone for what would be an unforgettable stay. It was a bit more eventful than I had anticipated. As our plane descended, the unmistakable pull of turbulence rocked us back and forth. We were mere moments from touching down when the pilot suddenly pulled up, the engines roaring as we soared back into the sky. The cabin filled with an uncomfortable silence— everyone glancing around as if to ask, 'Was that supposed to happen?' My heart, firmly lodged in my stomach, thumped wildly as the pilot calmly explained the situation: the winds were too strong for a safe landing. We would circle for a bit, wait for the winds to die down, and try again.

That moment of pulling up instead of touching down— hearts in throats, plans suddenly up in the air—was a masterclass in handling the unexpected. In the tense silence that filled the cabin, I realized something about our relationship with control. While we passengers gripped our seats and held our breath, the pilot's calm voice carried the confidence of someone who knew exactly when to change course. It struck me that true skill isn't about powering through at all costs, but about recognizing when conditions aren't right and having the courage to hit pause. Sometimes the bravest thing isn't pushing forward—it's knowing when to step back, reset, and wait for a better moment.

Fifteen minutes later, the plane touched down with smooth precision, and we breathed a collective sigh of relief. That sense of shared vulnerability faded quickly, replaced by excitement as we prepared to explore what this remarkable country had to offer.

It didn't take long for the country's charm to reveal itself. Everywhere we went, we were met with genuine warmth. It felt like being kind was the national way of life. Filipinos have a way of making you feel welcome in an utterly sincere manner, almost as though they've been waiting for you to arrive just so they could show you a good time.

One of the most unexpected and heartwarming moments came during a stay at a small beachfront hotel. Next door, a lively celebration was taking place, and after some friendly inquiries, I learned it was a pre-wedding party. The revellers, many of whom were staying just for one night, had gone all out with food, decorations, and music. After a brief conversation with one of the family members, I congratulated them and thought nothing of it. Fifteen minutes later, I was handed a formal invitation to the wedding for our family of 4.

I was taken aback.

We had just literally met fifteen minutes ago and now we were going to the wedding. As much as we wanted to attend, it wouldn't work logistically, but as a token of their hospitality, they later brought us several slices of their celebratory engagement cake. It was a small gesture, but one that spoke volumes about the generosity and openness of the Filipino people. Here, we weren't just tourists—we were guests, embraced as part of their community, if only for a fleeting moment.

In every encounter, I found myself marvelling at how Filipinos treated us—visitors from halfway across the world—as though we were part of their extended family. I often joked with the locals, trying to lighten the formality with which they addressed us. The girls were especially amused by how often we were referred to as Sir and Madam, titles that seemed far too grand for us. But this was just part of their nature—a deep-seated respect for guests, no matter who they were or where they came from. Much to everyone's amusement, I butchered the occasional phrase in Tagalog, their national language, but even in my linguistic stumbles, they found joy. They laughed with me and those moments reminded me of how universal humour and connection can be.

The Philippines takes hospitality to a new level. On one of our flights between islands, we experienced this firsthand. As we disembarked, the flight crew handed out umbrellas—not because it was raining, but to shield us from the blazing sun for the short walk—about 30 seconds from the base of the stairs on the tarmac to the terminal. It wasn't something we had asked for, nor even expected, but there it was—hospitality so thoughtful it extended to moments most people would overlook. It was as if they were saying, 'We've thought of everything for your comfort, even from the sun.'

Apparently, there's a saying that you can tell a lot about a culture by how they treat their animals. It seemed that every household had at least one pet—most had several. Filipinos' love for animals was everywhere from dogs and cats to birds and even fish. In Manila, we visited a mall that actively encouraged patrons to bring their pets inside, provided they followed a strict set of guidelines: pets had to wear an ID badge on their collar, be on a leash at all times, and wear diapers.

Yes, that's right—diapers.

We could have spent all day there, just watching impeccably dressed dogs stroll through the aisles as their owners proudly showed them off like they were celebrities. The girls were in stitches, and honestly, so was I. Who knew a trip to the mall could turn into a full-fledged pet fashion show?

Basketball, too, has a special place in Filipino culture. Despite what some might call a national height disadvantage, it's a sport beloved by almost everyone. Whenever we told Filipinos we were from Toronto, the response was almost always the same: "The Raptors—they won the championships in 2019!" Filipinos, while aware that they may not be the tallest, don't let this discourage them from fully engaging in the game. Courts could be found in nearly every neighbourhood, with kids playing pickup games well into the evening. The passion they had for basketball mirrored their zest for life—unbridled, energetic, and always with a sense of fun.

What's beautiful about how Filipinos embrace basketball is that they don't get caught up in the usual excuses. Sure, they might not have the average height of other nations, but that's beside the point. They jump into the game with everything they've got because they understand something deeper — that the real loss would be standing on the sidelines, too afraid to play at all. It's this refusal to be discouraged that appealed to me. They'd rather be in the game, giving it their all, than wondering 'what if?'

One of our favourite pastimes during our stay was the 'how many people can you fit on a motorcycle' game. No matter where we went, we were amazed by how many passengers a single motorcycle could carry. The record we witnessed was a family of five: Dad, two kids, a mother clutching what looked like a newborn for dear life, and chickens in baskets hanging off the sides. It was a sight to behold, one that left the girls in utter disbelief. I explained to the girls that motorcycles weren't just transportation in this part of the world; they were a way of life, and everyone did their best to make it work.

One of the most remarkable spots we visited was Virgin Island—a pristine sandbar in the middle of the Pacific that plays a daily vanishing act with the ocean. This natural wonder completely disappears underwater twice a day, which means timing is everything. We were fortunate to arrive just as the tides had pulled back, revealing this temporary slice of paradise. Picture postcard perfection: crystal clear water meeting powdery white sand, stretching out before us. We spent our time basking in the sun, collecting seashells, and simply absorbing the beauty of it all. But nature was already taking back what was hers. We watched, fascinated, as the water gradually crept higher, the ocean slowly erasing our perfect little beach from view. Before long, our temporary paradise was slipping back beneath the waves—a mesmerizing reminder of nature's perpetual dance with time and tide.

Yet, not every moment was lighthearted. One afternoon, while wading through the warm waters of a remote island, I stepped on a sea urchin. These sea creatures have movable spines that they use to defend themselves from things like.....my foot. As I stepped, I felt a sharp pain but brushed it off, thinking it was nothing serious. Hours later, however, the pain hadn't subsided, so I asked the front desk at our hotel for advice. Within minutes, I was being whisked off to a local clinic. The doctor treated me with such care and concern that I felt like I was his only patient despite the clinic being packed with ill patients. His calm demeanour and genuine interest in my well-being stood out, and I couldn't help but reflect on how rare such personalized care can be.

One thing that immediately stands out in the Philippines is just how much they love Western pop culture, and it's everywhere. Instead of the usual boring boarding music, one airline decided to turn things up a notch with Taylor Swift's biggest hits. And, wow, did it make for a memorable flight! We were some of the first passengers onboard, and watching everyone else enter was a show in itself. It was as if Taylor had joined the flight in person. Passengers were 'shaking it off' down the aisles, lipsyncing like they were auditioning for a music video. One guy even gave Ayana a high-five and said, "You're a Swiftie too!" She was grinning from ear to ear.

Filipinos' dedication to pop culture goes all out. Not only does every top hit play endlessly, but there's also a local cover version by a Filipino artist. Some cover songs are so spot on that we'd play a little game to guess whether it was the original singer or a talented local.

And karaoke?

It's practically the national pastime—there are as many karaoke bars as there are palm trees. I can only imagine what the scene looks like at a 'Filipinos' Got Talent' audition. While the joy of karaoke and pop culture was everywhere, it was just one facet of what made the Philippines special. What truly stayed with us was something deeper.

Perhaps the most poignant lesson we learned during our time in the Philippines was that happiness, and generosity don't depend on material wealth.

As we travelled from one island to another, we encountered people living in circumstances that were far removed from the comforts we often take for granted. Yet, despite the visible poverty, the warmth and spirit of the people never faltered. There was a contentment in their simplicity, a joy in their everyday lives that reminded us of the things that truly matter.

Perhaps that's the true gift of travel—not just discovering new places, but learning how to make others feel at home, wherever you go.

Key Takeaways

1. Value of Genuine Connections: Seek to create meaningful relationships with others, regardless of their background or circumstances.

2. Embrace Simplicity: Appreciate the joy in simple moments and interactions, recognizing that happiness often comes from connections rather than material possessions.

3. Cultivate a Spirit of Family: Strive to make others feel welcomed and valued in your life, fostering a sense of community and support.

Key Questions

1. How do the attitudes of others shape your experience in unfamiliar environments, and how can you cultivate a similar warmth in your own community?

2. What moments of connection have you experienced in your own life that reminded you of the importance of kindness and generosity?

PAUSE & REFLECT: Cultivating Connection

1. Practice Generosity

   TODAY: Reach out to someone you've been meaning to connect with.

   THIS WEEK: Host a gathering where each guest brings someone new.

   THIS MONTH: Establish a welcoming ritual at home or in the workplace.

2. Break Social Barriers

   - Strike up a conversation with someone you don't know well.

   - Share a meal with people outside your usual social circle.

   - Volunteer to assist in your community.

3. Build Lasting Bonds

   - Start a tradition in your neighborhood.

   - Create opportunities for shared experiences.

   - Document and celebrate the connections you make.

Taking the leap, one splash at a time!

Who says you can't mix business with pleasure?

Every step is a reminder that life is better by the sea.

Manila shines brightest under the night sky.

Kasia with a drink in hand, ocean in sight—living her best life.

Propelling into paradise, one island at a time.

Little architect, big ambitions.

Soaking in the Manila skyline views.

When the journey is as beautiful as the destination.

Turquoise waters and tranquil vibes.

CHAPTER #6
NEW ZEALAND

"There's no need to go to any other country when
New Zealand has everything."
– Rhys Darby

New Zealand, or Aotearoa, as it's known by its Maori
name, swept us off our feet with its breathtaking
landscapes and the seamless integration of its
indigenous Māori culture into everyday life. From the
moment we set foot in the country, it was clear that
this was a place that honoured its roots. We saw it
everywhere: street names written in both English and
Māori, schoolchildren actively learning about traditional
customs, and public spaces adorned with Māori art
and symbols. It was as if the entire country had woven
its culture into the very fabric of daily life, making it
impossible not to notice and appreciate.

This wasn't just about checking a box for cultural
awareness; it felt deeply genuine. Museums across the
country celebrated Māori history and art, giving both

locals and visitors a window into the rich heritage that shaped the land. It was inspiring to see how a country could integrate its indigenous roots into the present day, making it a living, breathing part of everyday life. For our children, it was a powerful lesson in respect, inclusion, and the importance of preserving culture.

From the very first interaction, it was clear that New Zealand wasn't simply a tourist destination; it was a place that invited you to be part of its story. The Māori values of manaakitanga (hospitality), whanaungatanga (relationship-building), and kaitiakitanga (guardianship of the land) were evident in every encounter we had.

Our adventure began in Wellington, where I had a comical experience with the local car rental agency. I took the short ten-minute walk from our Airbnb to the rental office, enjoying the brisk air and a rare moment of solitude. Once inside, I noticed all the rental companies were packed into one tiny room—a clever use of space, I thought. After waiting a bit, I rang the bell for help. To my surprise, the woman who'd been working at another car agency across the room a moment earlier casually strolled over, swapped her name tag, and greeted me as the representative for my agency. I burst out laughing, but she couldn't understand the humour in the whole thing, which made me uncontrollably laugh even more. It felt like a Monty Python sketch or as if I was on Candid

Camera. She had seen me looking around, wondering who would be staffing my agency's counter, but just kept tapping away at her keyboard until I tapped the bell for assistance. With the car keys finally in hand, I calmed down, and we set off to explore both the north and south islands of the country, embarking on scenic drives that we would talk about for years to come.

Our visit to the Te Papa Tongarewa Museum in Wellington offered a profound dive into the Māori culture and history. This national museum seamlessly blended storytelling, artifacts, and interactive displays, capturing the essence of the Māori people and their legacy. One exhibit that particularly resonated with us showcased a beautifully carved meeting house, where the intricate details told stories of ancestors and the spiritual connection between people and the land. The kids were captivated by the multimedia presentations that brought these tales to life, and we left with a deeper understanding of the cultural heartbeat that has shaped New Zealand's identity.

The drive from Wellington to the picturesque coastal town of New Plymouth felt like entering a whole new world. The winding roads, with their dense greenery and occasional glimpses of the sea, felt like an open invitation to explore. We were welcomed with open arms by Virginia, a dear friend of the kids' Great-

Grandma, Betty—whom they affectionately called GG. Virginia and Betty's friendship dated back decades to a European bus tour in the '90s, and despite the miles between them, they managed to keep their bond alive through handwritten letters and the occasional visit. Though GG isn't with us anymore, it truly felt like she was with us in spirit as we exchanged stories and sipped cup after cup of English Breakfast tea with Virginia. Between lakeside strolls and bountiful feasts, Virginia's hospitality was boundless. It was a beautiful reminder that friendships have the power to bridge not only time and distance but also generations. Who would have thought that a random meeting on a bus all those years ago would lead to our kids connecting with GG's old travel buddy on the other side of the world?

When I think back and reflect whether it was meeting my grandparents during one of my first visits to Ghana, the birth of my daughters, or getting married all of my clearest memories come from moments when I finally stopped running. Here in Virginia's home, taking in the beautiful views of the Tasman Sea, I'm struck by how the most meaningful moments often come when we just... stop.

Stop rushing.

Stop planning.

Stop trying to squeeze meaning from every second.

Like that chance meeting between GG and Virginia on a European bus—neither of them was trying to forge a lifelong friendship that would touch their grandchildren and great-grandchildren. They were just present, open to whatever the moment might bring. Watching these kids now, soaking in Virginia's stories over tea, I'm reminded that sometimes the deepest connections form not when we're charging forward, but when we allow ourselves time to just stop and pause. Maybe that's what GG and Virginia understood all along—that life's sweetest chapters often begin when we have the courage to pause, to let the world catch up with us as opposed to us constantly catching up with the world.

In Rotorua, we had the chance to watch a traditional Māori performance, where performers in striking attire showcased a blend of powerful chants and rhythmic movements. The energy in the room was palpable, with each movement and chant conveying pride and deep cultural significance. Our daughters sat wide-eyed, taking in the spectacle as history and tradition came to life before them. It wasn't just a performance; it was a moment of cultural immersion that highlighted the strength and unity of the Māori people and added depth to our visit.

Travelling across the North Island, we found ourselves in Waihi Beach (pronounced Wah-hee), a coastal paradise with endless blue waters so stunning they would make a mermaid blush. During a morning stroll around town, I stumbled upon a quirky spot called the Menz Shed. Naturally, my curiosity led me inside, where I found a group of retired gentlemen swapping stories while working on community projects. Just my luck—I had arrived right in time for tea and biscuits. Of course, my phone was back at the Airbnb, tucked away for an impromptu digital detox, so Janice's calls went unanswered. She was left imagining the worst—perhaps thinking that I'd been swept away by a flock of sheep. After all, fun fact: New Zealand has more sheep than people.

Meanwhile, I entertained my new Kiwi friends with stories of my Canadian and Ghanaian roots. To my surprise, many of them had ties to Canada, including one man who'd gotten married in Toronto half a century ago. Despite their 'Menz Shed' moniker, these fellas were young at heart, teasing each other—and me—like I was a clueless Canuck who'd wandered into their midst. I played along, which made them laugh even harder. The whole scene was an excellent reminder that no matter where you are in the world, a sense of humour can make any situation feel like home.

You know it intuitively but it's amazing to be reminded how laughter is this universal key that unlocks doors we didn't even know were closed. Sitting there in that Menz Shed, trading jabs with my Kiwi mates who could've been my uncles or cousins back home, it hit me— we're all just looking for that spark of recognition in each other's eyes. Here I was, this guy from thousands of miles from anywhere I'd call familiar, yet somehow feeling like I'd stumbled into my own backyard. It's funny how we humans work—we spend so much time building structures around what differentiates us, when really, it's in those moments of shared laughter, those jokes that somehow work across continents, that we connect with our true selves. Maybe that's the real magic of travel—not in the places we visit, but in the tiny moments that change our perspective. It's realizing that 'foreign' is simply another word for 'a friend we haven't laughed with yet.'

Our visit to the Waitomo Glowworm Caves took us into an entirely different world—one that was both eerie and mesmerizing. These are a series of limestone caves on the country's North Island, famous for the thousands of tiny glowworms that illuminate the underground tunnels with an enchanting blue-green glow. To explore the caves, we had to crouch down low in several areas, sometimes barely fitting through openings that were only about 90 cm (35 inches) high. The low ceilings forced us into a near crawl, making the whole experience feel like an adventure from the get-go. But nothing prepared us for the boat ride that followed.

Once inside the cave, we were guided onto a small boat in total darkness. The only light came from the glowworms scattered across the ceiling, their tiny lights creating a galaxy above us. We were warned not to stick our hands out of the boat lest we accidentally touch or disturb the glowworms. It was eerie being in that darkness; our senses heightened as we floated along. What truly surprised us was the guide's ability to navigate the boat without any visible markers. It wasn't until later that we learned the secret—a rope system allowed her to pull the boat along in the pitch-black cave. One of the kids' well-meaning but humorous questions about whether eating a glowworm would make a person glow was met with a firm no. The whole experience felt like something out of a dream, a surreal mixture of awe and wonder.

On the southern island, the stretch of road from Queenstown to Glenorchy is said to be one of the most scenic drives in the world, and it certainly lived up to its reputation. We weaved our way along the cliffs, with dramatic views of Lake Wakatipu below, each turn offering an even more stunning vista. At one point, we had to come to a screeching halt as a tourist lay flat in the middle of the road to get that perfect shot of the lake. I couldn't believe it and neither did the rest of the family. The shock of someone lying in the middle of a busy two-lane highway for a picture was mind-boggling, and yet, somehow, it felt like such a New Zealand moment. Despite the minor scare, we carried on, fully immersed in the beauty around us.

Beyond its scenic beauty, New Zealand, the world's go-to destination for extreme sports, invited us to dive into some unforgettable local thrills. We'd heard about zorbing—a hilarious activity that our girls absolutely had to try. Watching them roll downhill inside a giant inflatable ball, head over heels with water splashing everywhere and their laughter filling the air, was pure joy. Ayana, the bravest of the bunch, insisted on several rounds, each one more daring than the last. Janice and I thought this clearly seemed a sport best suited for the young, but our 'old soul' attitude was quickly checked when a rather elderly lady emerged from one of the inflatable balls, grinning ear-to-ear, proving that a bit of thrill knows no age limit.

Jet boating, another adrenaline-packed activity, had us skimming across shallow rivers at dizzying speeds, twisting and turning with what seemed like millimetre precision. There were moments when we were certain we were going to crash into the rocks or trees, but the boat's captain expertly manoeuvred us out of every tight spot. The thrill was contagious, and we all found ourselves giddy despite the heart-pounding intensity of the ride.

After the thrill of jet boating on the river, we moved on to explore the bungee jumping platform and ziplining activity, eager to continue to soak in the atmosphere of adventure. As we approached the viewing deck for bungee jumping, we were taken aback by an unexpected sight—a young man standing confidently in nothing but his birthday suit, ready to take the leap. What should have been a routine adrenaline rush suddenly turned into a surreal spectacle, leaving us all blinking in disbelief. It felt less like an adventure sport and more like we'd accidentally stumbled into a nudist retreat.

The reactions from the crowd were priceless—gasps, giggles, and plenty of wide-eyed shock. Even I, having seen my fair share of oddities on this trip, found myself laughing along with everyone else. His family, clearly trying to be encouraging, cheered him on and a nearby group of seniors revelled in the unexpected entertainment. One elderly lady rubbing her eyes and elbowing Janice for clarification inquired, "Is he really naked?" Janice explained that he was, and she retorted, "I guess my eyesight isn't what it used to be!" I chuckled to myself, wondering if there was something in the water 'down under' that made people so comfortable in their birthday suits. First that cheerful fellow in Maroochydore giving his morning "G'day mate!" in full glory, and now this daredevil taking naked bungee jumping to new heights. At this rate, I half expected our next zipline instructor to show up wearing nothing but a helmet and a smile. Some people really take 'letting it all hang out' quite literally.

One of the highlights of our New Zealand adventure was the All Blacks Rugby Experience Tour in Auckland, where we got a crash course in what it means to be part of this legendary team. The kids were all in doing their own form of the haka—a traditional Māori war dance performed to display strength and unity. It's meant to intimidate opponents before the game and fire up the team, and let me tell you, it works. We faced off against a 3D projection of the current All Blacks team, chanting back and forth. Even knowing they weren't real didn't stop the chills; those holograms meant business! Then came the rugby toss, which turned out to be an absolute blast. We all took turns throwing and catching, feeling like pros—until we realized just how much coordination it takes to excel at this game. But hey, we had fun, and for a moment, we were honorary All Blacks... or at least we like to think so.

As we continued our travels through New Zealand, the country revealed more of its unique character. Unlike Australia, where dangerous animals are a constant topic of conversation, New Zealand had none of those concerns. The only 'danger' here seemed to be the winding roads, which twisted and turned so often that cruise control became useless. But what really added to the adventure were the countless one-way roads. These narrow stretches felt like an ongoing game of chicken as we navigated single-lane roads where only one vehicle could pass at a time in either direction. Each approach became a silent negotiation of who would back up or push forward first. It required constant focus, and by the end of each journey, my arms were a little sore, but the thrill of navigating such roads became a unique part of the New Zealand experience.

And if that wasn't enough, New Zealand seemed to have a national obsession with orange pylons. Seriously, I don't know who's running the pylon business or who they're related to in government, but it's impressive. Even on perfectly fine roads with no visible construction, there they were—standing proudly, guarding stretches of highway like tiny, fluorescent soldiers. It felt like a scavenger hunt we hadn't signed up for, as we spotted them in the most random, untouched spots. By the end of the trip, we started taking bets on how far we'd go before seeing another cluster of traffic cones. New Zealand: where the roads keep you alert, and the pylons keep you guessing.

This country left a lasting impression on us, not only because of its jaw-dropping scenery and thrilling adventures but also because of the way it seamlessly intertwined its past with its present. The Māori culture wasn't just something to observe—it was something to be lived, respected, and appreciated. In a way, New Zealand's approach to honouring its indigenous heritage mirrored our own journey: it wasn't about passing through; it was about fully immersing ourselves in each experience, learning, and growing as we went along.

Key Takeaways

1. Embrace Cultural Integration: Incorporate diverse cultural perspectives into your daily life to enrich your understanding of the world.

2. Seek Adventure: Look for opportunities to try new things and push your limits, fostering personal growth and creativity.

3. Cultivate Resilience and Humour: Approach challenges with a light-hearted attitude to make the journey more enjoyable and fulfilling.

Key Questions

1. When faced with unexpected challenges in your journey—be they physical, emotional, or logistical— how do you maintain a sense of humour and resilience? What strategies can you adopt to navigate these moments while finding meaning in the experience?

2. What steps can you take to better understand and honour the cultures you encounter?

PAUSE & REFLECT: Discovering Your Own Backyard

1. Explore Local Treasures

    TODAY: Find three moments to truly stop and observe what's happening around you without reaching for your phone

    THIS WEEK: Visit a place in your community where time moves slower—a garden, library, or quiet café

    THIS MONTH: Create regular "pause points" in your schedule where you can be fully present without an agenda

2. Create Family Rituals

    •   Create "curiosity walks" where each person takes turns choosing an unexpected turn

    •   Start rituals that make ordinary moments feel special—Sunday morning window shopping, full moon picnics, or first-frost hot chocolate

    •   Document your discoveries through any medium that brings you joy—sketching, writing, photography, or collecting small treasures

3. Connect With Your Community

    •   Support independent businesses and get to know the people behind them

    •   Participate in community decision-making through local meetings and initiatives

    •   Create or join projects that beautify and care for shared spaces

A calm lake perfectly mirrors the sky and mountains.

Art comes alive in Christchurch.

Enjoying a walk along the promenade in New Plymouth.

Ayana enthusiastically throws a rugby ball at a high-tech interactive display.

Enjoying some quiet time in the neighbourhood library.

Gliding through the majestic Milford Sound.

Honouring tradition through dance.

Kasia hopping gracefully along the rocks.

Janice and the kids soaking in mountain views on a crisp, clear day.

Taking in the breathtaking Milford Sound with the kids.

Taking the plunge fearless, free
and naked!

Towering peaks of Milford
Sound.

CHAPTER #7
GHANA

"I am not African because I was born in Africa. I am African because Africa was born in me." – Former Ghanaian President Kwame Nkrumah

---

Returning to my ancestral homeland as an adult has been a transformative experience—one that is deeply personal and meaningful in ways I could never have imagined in my youth. This time, however, the journey carries even more weight because I'm sharing it with my spouse and children.

There's something profoundly enriching about watching my daughters absorb the vibrant culture and history of Ghana, a place that is so much a part of me and them.

It's allowed me to view my own past and Ghana's history of independence with fresh eyes. In the past, I didn't fully appreciate the significance of that independence— the struggles and triumphs that shaped this land and the people who call it home. But as I've matured and moved through the stages of adulthood, Ghana's history is something I've come to feel deeply connected to. It's become front and center in my mind as I reflect on what this country means not just for me but for my children and for future generations.

I grew up in a large extended family, especially on my mother's side. She was the second youngest of eleven children, with a significant age gap between her and the eldest sibling. On my father's side, he was the eldest of four. His father's passing when he was just in his twenties weighed heavily on him, shaping the serious, stoic demeanour I've come to associate with him, being the eldest boy and by default the 'man of the house.' My father shouldered a weight of responsibility at an age when most people are still figuring out their place in the world.

In contrast, my mother, being the youngest girl in a large, affluent family, had a more carefree approach to life. She possessed a certain joie de vivre that made her laugh off most situations, no matter how challenging they might seem. I never fully understood how their respective upbringings influenced their parenting styles until I stood on the soil where their stories began. The often-quoted statement of 'it takes a village to raise a child' was the epitome of my childhood. When I reflect on my younger years, it's only now that I realize that the vast majority of my initial friend network was in fact the Ghana community in Ottawa, where I grew up. In my family, there's an ongoing joke with my kids: whenever I introduce someone as an 'aunt,' 'uncle,' or 'cousin,' they quietly ask me, "Are they actually related to us or are they just pretend relatives?"

You see, in Ghanaian culture, the word 'family' expands to include anyone who brings joy, laughter, and an occasional pinch of playful mischief to your life.

One of the most moving parts of our trip was visiting the ancestral homes of both my parents. Walking through the places where they spent their youth, hearing their stories, and retracing their steps to Canada added a new layer of understanding. I realized how their paths, while shaped by hardship and privilege in equal measure, had prepared them for the life they eventually built. The contrast between their backgrounds became clearer as I listened to the anecdotes of their youth—my mother's bustling life in a large family and my father's early responsibilities after the loss of his father. Those stories connected me not only to them but to Ghana, reminding me that our personal histories are inextricably linked to this land. It was a humbling realization.

In those moments of shared laughter, meals, and time spent together, surrounded by the warmth of extended family, I felt the true essence of home. Having my entire family in Ghana, with my siblings and parents all under one roof, made it even more special. I recognized how fleeting these opportunities are, especially as the years go by. It became important to me to slow down, to be present, and to absorb each moment in its entirety. These rare chances to connect with family, especially in Ghana, are precious, and I knew they would become fewer and farther between.

Funny how time sneaks up on you like that. There I was in Ghana, surrounded by family, when it hit me—these weren't just regular family hangouts anymore. Each moment felt like finding something precious, something you want to cup in your hands and keep safe forever. I had to travel all the way to Ghana to figure out what I should've known all along— that home isn't about walls and addresses. It's hiding in the belly laughs around the dinner table, in those stories that get better with each retelling, in those perfect little moments when you look around and think, 'Yeah, I want to freeze this exactly how it is right now.'

As we moved through Ghana, one of the most striking changes I noticed was the increasing presence of foreign diaspora visiting the country. Ghana, a coastal nation along the Atlantic Ocean, was once a major hub for the British slave trade, with countless Africans transported to South America, the Caribbean, and the United States. In recent years, there's been a concerted effort to encourage descendants, particularly African Americans, to retrace their roots. This movement has brought a surge of visitors, contributing to the country's tourism and foreign investment boom. On previous trips, I don't recall seeing as many Americans as I did this time. Their presence is unmistakable now, and they bring with them not only a connection to their ancestry but also an influx of energy and resources.

While this resurgence of interest in Ghana is positive in many ways, it's not without its challenges. The high cost of living, particularly in urban areas, has risen dramatically, placing a strain for many Ghanaians who are already struggling to make ends meet. This is especially evident during the Christmas season, when throngs of tourists flood the country as the dry season commences. During this time, large swaths of the diaspora return to celebrate the holidays, driving prices to astronomical levels and making it even more difficult for locals to afford basic necessities. It's a tension I felt deeply as I moved through the country, seeing the juxtaposition of foreign investment and local hardship.

Despite these challenges, I see Ghana as a land brimming with untapped potential. My personal and professional travels have given me a global perspective, and I no longer see Ghana's struggles as insurmountable. Instead of feeling frustrated or resigned to the difficulties the country faces, I feel empowered to contribute in some way. Though I was born in Canada, with all the privileges and opportunities that come with it, I feel a deep connection to Ghana's future. I can no longer sit idly by, waiting for others to effect change. It's not about being a saviour; it's about figuring out how I use my resources, my ideas, and my experience to help move the country forward.

Growing up, Ghana was like this treasured photo— something to look at, to remember, to show others. But now, standing here as an adult, it feels more like a conversation I need to be part of. Not in that save-the-world kind of way—we've all seen how that story goes.

This is different.

It's like when you finally learned to drive and suddenly realize you can help with the family road trips. You're not taking over; you're just adding your strength to the journey. Maybe that's what it means to really grow up— when you stop seeing problems as someone else's to fix and start thinking, 'Hey, I've got something to bring to the table.'

These thoughts became especially poignant during this visit as I watched my children begin to appreciate the land of their ancestors. Kasia and Ayana are now old enough to absorb the culture, the history, and the challenges of Ghana. I want them to see the potential I see here, to understand that this country, too, is part of their identity. Our visit this time was a careful balance of education and enjoyment, with moments of reflection on the country's challenges as well as the lighter, more joyous aspects of life here.

Visiting the country's first presidential library, belonging to the country's first president, Kwame Nkrumah, was incredibly insightful. I wanted my children to understand the significance of Ghana being the first sub-Saharan country to gain independence from its colonial rulers, the British. As we moved through the exhibits, I shared what I knew, but it was the visual history that really captured their attention.

They chuckled at pictures of President Nkrumah dancing with Queen Elizabeth II and marvelled at the donation President John F. Kennedy made to Nkrumah—a 1961 Cadillac, rumoured to be part of an effort to sway the Ghanaian leader toward capitalist ideals. Whether or not it worked, we all know that Nkrumah was eventually ousted in a coup d'état, reportedly with some assistance from the CIA, while he was on a peacekeeping mission in

Vietnam in the 1960s. The layers of history are complex, and I wondered how much of it would stay with the girls as they grew older.

During the trip, the girls learned that names hold special value, too; each child is named based on the day they're born. For instance, my Ghanaian name is Kwesi (pronounced 'Kway-see') because I'm a boy born on Sunday. Janice is Afua (pronounced 'Ah-foo-wah') because she's a girl born on Friday, like Ayana. The former UN Secretary General Kofi Annan was a boy born on Friday. It's hard to believe, but one-seventh of the Ghanaian population shares the same name! At large family gatherings you can imagine the confusion when someone calls one of these names and so many of us turn around thinking it's for us. Besides day-based names, many have English or Christian names in addition to also being named after a family member. For example, Kasia is named after my Mom in the traditional Ghanaian sense—her Ghanaian name is Adjoa Obiri (pronounced 'Ah-jew-wah Oh-bur-ree'). It's complicated but fascinating.

Not all our lessons were as serious. One of the more humorous aspects of the trip was watching my father, integrate his own unique brand of teaching into our homeschooling routine. Papa, or 'Papa Beard' as the girls fondly call him, decided to reward the girls for writing book reports on the stories they read during the trip. For each report, he promised them a crisp five-dollar bill—a sweet deal, especially for Kasia, who saw an opportunity to turn her love of reading into a little entrepreneurial venture. Kasia, the diligent student, took the assignment seriously and crafted thoughtful and detailed reports. Ayana, however, had a different approach. She saw the promise of easy money and decided to shortcut the process.

Papa, who had perhaps anticipated another thorough analysis, was pleasantly surprised by the report's succinctness and general clarity. He praised Ayana for her work, and she beamed with pride, fully expecting to see her earnings materialize soon. But Kasia, ever the truthteller and perhaps a bit miffed by the apparent ease with which her sister had completed the assignment, couldn't resist pointing out that Ayana's book report summary bore a striking resemblance to the summary at the back of the book. "Papa," she said, with a slight tone of indignation, "Ayana didn't write that. She just copied it!" The room fell silent as all eyes turned to Ayana, whose grin had started to fade. Papa, trying to maintain his composure, gave a slow nod and said, "Well, Ayana, that's a good lesson. You've got to do the work yourself if you want to get paid."

One of the most enjoyable hands-on activities was making chocolate. Despite knowing that Ghana is one of the largest exporters of chocolate and gold, I had never experienced chocolate-making firsthand. Bioko Chocolates offered us a fantastic opportunity to see how chocolate is made from the cocoa bean through to the final product. Though I'm not a chocolate lover—I know, a cardinal sin for many—the experience was thoroughly enjoyable under the hot African sun. We each created our own chocolate squares, filled with a variety of nuts, chili pepper, raisins, and whatever else our hearts desired. The girls loved it.

As we ended our time in Ghana, I reflected on the significance of this trip. Watching my children connect with their heritage in such a meaningful way filled me with optimism for their future. This journey was about more than sightseeing—it was about identity, roots, and the power of family. It reminded me that while my life may have taken me far from Ghana, my connection to this land is as strong as ever.

Key Takeaways

1. Responsibility and Empowerment: Recognizing the potential for positive change in your community encourages a proactive approach to challenges.

2. Cultural Roots: Understanding our cultural roots deepens our connection to family and heritage, enriching our identity.

3. Resilience and Opportunity: Recognizing the struggles and triumphs of our ancestors can inspire resilience and motivate us to seize opportunities for growth.

Key Questions

1. When you reflect on your parents, in what ways have your parents' backgrounds shaped your upbringing and values?

2. How does your heritage influence your identity and sense of belonging?

3. What wisdom from elders guides you today?

PAUSE & REFLECT: Roots, Identity, and Legacy

1. Connect With Your Roots

   TODAY: Call a family member and ask about your family history

   THIS WEEK: Document a family tradition you want to preserve

   THIS MONTH: Create a new ritual that honours your heritage

2. Expand Your Definition of Family

   • Identify those who feel like family beyond blood relations

   • Reconnect with an old friend who has always felt like family

   • Research your family name's origin

3. Consider Your Legacy

   • Reflect on the impact you want to have on those around you

   • Explore one meaningful way to contribute to your community

   • Preserve stories and wisdom by recording conversations with family members or mentors

A quiet moment remembering those who came before us.

Exploring the vibrant market scene.

Dad and I taking a dip to beat the heat.

Taking in the legacy at the Kwame Nkrumah Presidential Museum—
an inspiring piece of history.

Wandering through grandma's village, a place full of history.

CHAPTER #8
ALBANIA

"Simplicity is the ultimate sophistication."
– Leonardo da Vinci

Albania was the one country on our journey that raised the most eyebrows. It was unusual in that so few people we knew had ever travelled there or knew much about it. As is typical of human nature, we often create preconceived notions based on what we think we know about a place or hear through the media. This allows us to fill in the blanks and move on without digging deeper to uncover the facts. But Albania was a delightful surprise. In my mind, it's the true hidden gem of Europe. The landscape and scenery were absolutely stunning. The coastline along the Adriatic and Ionian seas was sublime, offering breathtaking views at every turn. The rugged mountains, pristine beaches, and lush green valleys seemed almost too beautiful to be real. As we traversed this land, each vista revealed a new layer of its natural splendour, making it clear why this country deserves more attention.

The food was equally remarkable. We indulged in a wide variety of fresh fish, meats, and other local dishes. Traditional Albanian cuisine, with its emphasis on fresh, locally-sourced ingredients, provided a feast for the senses. Yet, beyond the delicious meals, our experience with Albanian hospitality made me rethink what service really means.

Back home in North America, we're used to a certain dance in restaurants and hotels — the friendly greetings, the check-ins, the 'how is everything tasting?' It's our way of doing things, and it can be lovely when genuine. But sometimes these exchanges feel more like following a script than creating real connections. Being in Albania reminded me that hospitality comes in many flavors, and sometimes the most authentic service isn't wrapped in familiar packaging.

At first, this businesslike approach was strange, even uncomfortable. I found myself thinking, 'Why aren't they more friendly?' But after a few days, I began to appreciate it. There was something unusual about not needing to exchange perfunctory pleasantries every time I wanted a glass of water or asked for the bill.

This was an overall theme that persisted throughout our time in Albania. Interactions were direct, purposeful, and sometimes brusque but always efficient. It was a significant contrast to the North American style of hospitality, where waitstaff and shopkeepers in some cases engage in lengthy, convivial conversations with the expectation of a tip or a positive review at the end. In Albania, the focus was on the task at hand, and I came to realize that this was not due to a lack of hospitality but a different kind of hospitality—one that respected my time and theirs.

In fact, this experience gave me pause to reconsider the 'How are you?' culture that dominates in other parts of the world. Does the waiter really care how my day is going? In Albania, the exchange of services felt more honest in its simplicity. There was no rush to present the bill, no hovering to clear the table as soon as your fork hit the plate. In Albania, we were left to enjoy our meals at our own pace, which allowed us to savour both the food and the company without the pressure to finish and vacate the table for the next customer.

As we spent more time in the country, I began to piece together why Albanians might be this way. Much of it stems from its history, a past shaped by decades of isolation under a repressive regime. Enver Hoxha (pronounced n-ver ho-jah), the country's former head of state, ruled with an iron fist, preparing the nation for a possible invasion by littering the landscape with military bunkers. These bunkers, scattered throughout the countryside, are a stark reminder of a time when

Albania was one of the most isolated nations on Earth. The enemy never came, but the legacy of that paranoia remained. For decades, the Albanian people endured scarcity, suspicion, and fear, which shaped their interactions with the outside world. What I had initially perceived as indifference or coldness was perhaps a response to this history, where trust was a luxury few could afford.

The reserved nature of the people wasn't dissatisfaction or rudeness but rather a protective barrier built from years of hardship.

We ventured out to explore many of the military bunkers scattered across Albania's landscape, built during Hoxha's regime. The kids were fascinated by their sheer size and number, trying to imagine what life must have been like during that tense period. The juxtaposition of these relics of war against the serene natural beauty around them was striking, and it left a lasting impression on all of us.

A conversation with an older Albanian couple stood out to me in particular. Over coffee, I asked them about the reserved nature of the people I had encountered. They shared their perspective, reflecting on the country's tumultuous past. "We've lived through a lot. The past still lingers in our daily lives," they explained.

Their words gave me insight into how deeply historical experiences can shape present attitudes. It wasn't that Albanians didn't care—it was that they had learned to guard themselves.

This was particularly evident in the story the gentleman shared about his life. He had worked in the trades industry before the country was closed off from the world. Like many Albanians, he worked hard to make ends meet, and his job provided just enough for his family to get by. When the Berlin Wall fell and communism began to crumble, Albania, like many other countries, began to open up. The country needed a professional civil service to manage its governance structure and represent its interests abroad.

Despite his initial reluctance, the man's father encouraged him to tell himself a new story about his life. In other words, to take up the pen and become the author of a new chapter, refusing to let his past dictate his future path. Reluctantly, he explored a career in the foreign service, a choice that ultimately transformed his life, enabling him to transition into a new profession and eventually retire comfortably with a pension. His story reflected not only the resilience of the Albanian people but also their adaptability in the face of dramatic change.

You know what gets me about this man's story? That moment when his father basically said 'Hey, your old life doesn't get to decide your new one.' I mean, imagine that—there he was, hands rough from years of trade work, probably thinking 'This is just who I am,' when suddenly the whole world cracked open. Albania was changing, and his father saw something in him he couldn't yet see in himself. Or perhaps he could sense the changing tide and he wanted his son not to miss out on the opportunity the world was presenting to him.

It's wild how sometimes it takes someone else's belief in us to shake loose our own imagination of what's possible. Here's this guy who probably never pictured himself in a suit, working in the country's foreign service, and yet... he took that leap. Makes me think about all the stories we tell ourselves about who we are, and how quickly they can change when we dare to write a new page. Maybe that's the real courage—not the big career switch or even making it work—but that first moment of thinking 'Yeah, maybe I could be someone different.'

Tirana, Albania's vibrant capital, offers a unique blend of European charm and modern energy. One of the first things that struck me was how exceptionally clean the city is, with tree-lined boulevards and wide promenades filled with locals enjoying gelato and casual strolls. The city buzzes with life, filled with chaotic traffic that adds to its dynamic energy. Motorcycles weave through cars, while high-end vehicles dominate the streets, giving it an unmistakable sense of innovation and growth. If you didn't know better, you could easily mistake Tirana for one of Europe's major capitals like Paris, London, or Berlin. But in reality, this is one of the continent's most underrated cities, a hidden gem blending tradition and modernity.

The most entertaining part of driving in Albania is the parking. If you find a spot where you can squeeze your vehicle—even if it's sticking out into traffic—it's a parking spot. I was timid at first, not used to this wild, wild west of parking. But soon enough, I was kicking pylons out of the way and wedging our car into places that would make a Tetris champion proud. I'd see someone stop on a busy road, put on their hazards to pick up groceries or coffee, with all of us blaring our horns. Ten minutes later, they'd look out to see what the fuss was about, leisurely pack their bags in the trunk, and carry on like nothing happened. It's a unique blend of chaos and comedy, and somehow, it works.

A particular highlight of our Albanian journey was a day trip to Gjirokastra (pronounced gee-roh kas-trah), an ancient Ottoman town with stunning stone houses and steep cobblestone streets. We wandered through the town, marvelling at its architecture and the sweeping views of the surrounding valley. Exploring the town itself was a delight with its quiet, historical charm—it felt like we were stepping back in time. We stopped at a small café perched on the hillside, where we sipped local coffee and smoothies and soaked in the breathtaking scenery.

Swimming in the ancient waters of Lake Ohrid, one of Europe's deepest and oldest lakes, was an enjoyable experience. The lake's cool, crystal-clear waters were perfect for a refreshing swim, and we spent hours there enjoying the peace and quiet. The views across the lake, especially toward North Macedonia, were stunning. North Macedonia, a relatively obscure country for many travellers, revealed its breathtaking landscape from across the water. The entire experience was surreal, knowing we were swimming in a lake that had existed for millions of years.

There's a reason why those in the Mediterranean live longer. Yes, their diet plays a big role, but just as important is the way they move—they walk everywhere. It's a lifestyle that feels effortless yet profoundly intentional. We couldn't help but laugh when we arrived at our accommodations in southern Albania, dragging our luggage behind us. To use the elevator, we first had to climb a set of stairs to the first floor—a feature that seemed to completely defeat the purpose! But perhaps that's the point. Movement is woven into everyday life here, and it's a part of what makes this region so vibrant.

One tradition, in particular, stands out: xhiro (pronounced gy—roh). In Albanian, xhiro refers to the evening ritual of strolling—or a walk for the sake of walking or socializing—a custom I wish existed everywhere in the world. As soon as dusk falls and the oppressive heat of the day lifts, entire cities empty onto their piazzas and squares. Streets fill with people walking, chatting, and simply enjoying each other's company. It's a sight to behold.

During the day, these towns can feel almost deserted, and I often wondered how so few people actually lived here. Then I realized—they're inside, escaping the heat and saving their energy for the magic of the evening. When the sun sets, it's like the city comes alive. Glasses of Albanian red and white wine are raised in toasts, beer glasses are clinked, and coffee is savoured alongside scoops of creamy gelato. Kids kick soccer balls through the square, toddlers dart around giggling, and the air hums with a sense of joy and connection.

Here's what keeps hitting me about those Albanian evenings. We've somehow talked ourselves into believing connection needs a reason. Back home, we're all 'let's grab coffee next week' and 'we should schedule a walk,' while these folks just... show up.

Every. Single. Night.

It's like the whole city has this unspoken agreement: when the sun drops, we live. Not through Instagram stories or group chats, but with actual footsteps on stone, real wine in real glasses, kids' laughter bouncing off walls that have seen centuries of this same human dance.

Watching those streets come alive at dusk, I can't help but think we've overcomplicated everything. Here's this whole community that still remembers what we've forgotten— that maybe the best moments in life aren't the ones we plan. They're just the simple act of stepping outside, finding your people, and letting the evening unfold. No scheduling required, no purpose needed.

Trust me, the irony isn't lost on me. It took over a decade of meticulous planning—spreadsheets, savings accounts, and countless conversations about 'someday'—just to experience the beauty of a culture that thrives on unplanned moments.

In the end, our time in Albania was a journey of discovery, not just of a country but of a mindset. It reminded me that the allure of travel lies not in finding things that are familiar but in embracing the unfamiliar. With its stoic people and breathtaking landscapes, Albania challenged my perceptions and enriched my understanding of what it means to truly experience a place. From the rugged coastlines of the Adriatic to pristine lakes and mountains, the natural beauty here is nothing short of spectacular. I felt fortunate that we had the chance to witness this raw, unspoiled land before the inevitable influx of tourists, turning Albania into the next big travel destination. The quality of my time in this country wasn't diminished by the lack of overt friendliness; in fact, it added a layer of authenticity to our journey. The reserved demeanour of the people reflected a deeper history, one that had shaped their interactions with the world. And in the end, that authenticity—unpretentious and real—was what made Albania so memorable.

Key Takeaways

1. Travelling in unfamiliar environments prompts introspection about personal biases, expectations, and definitions of connection and friendliness.

2. Simple, unhurried moments—like an uninterrupted meal or a leisurely evening walk—can deepen our relationships and allow us to fully appreciate the present.

3. Cultural differences in hospitality remind us to appreciate the unique ways kindness is expressed, broadening our understanding of connection and generosity.

Key Questions

1. In what ways do I value simplicity in interactions, and how can I cultivate more meaningful exchanges without the need for superficial pleasantries?

2. What insights can I draw from my own experiences that may have mirrored Albania's journey from isolation to openness, and how can these lessons apply to my life today?

PAUSE & REFLECT: Authenticity and Adaptation

1. Discover Evening Rhythms

   TODAY: Take an evening walk in your neighborhood without your phone - notice how the community changes after sunset

   THIS WEEK: Create your own version of 'xhiro' - spend time in a public space with no agenda other than being present

   THIS MONTH: Start a sunset ritual in your community - invite neighbors for evening walks or gathering in local spaces

2. Appreciate Different Rhythms

   - Observe how people interact in an unfamiliar setting

   - Reflect on how history shapes a culture's guarded nature

3. Embrace Transformation

   - Share a story of overcoming adversity with a friend

   - Encourage someone to author a new chapter in their life

Capturing the magic of the
sunset at our place in Sarande.

Indulging in dessert after a
tasty Albanian feast.

Snacking on appetizers before
diving into the full spread.

Walking the beautiful Albanian
Riviera – where every step is a
view.

Discovering the history behind the bunkers in the Albanian countryside.

CHAPTER #9
SOUTH AFRICA

"To see through the eyes of a child is
to see truth unfiltered."
- Nelson Mandela

South Africa is an absolute enigma. Walking through the streets of its South West Township, Soweto, just outside of Johannesburg, the evidence of its complex history is unmistakable.

Just over 30 years ago, it would have been unfathomable for me to walk the streets of South Africa with a White wife and two mixed-race kids. As Trevor Noah so eloquently put it in his memoir, Born a Crime, our very existence would have been illegal.

It's astonishing to think that within my own lifetime—short as I may think it's been—such monumental shifts have taken place.

I wasn't sure how to feel about visiting South Africa at first. Janice had been eager to go on our honeymoon almost 15 years ago, but I wasn't ready to confront what had happened there. I worried about what might happen to a mixed-race couple in a country still finding its way, focusing on the potential for discomfort instead of seeing the beauty others told me about. In hindsight, I was fixated on the surface, reluctant to dig deeper into what was really going on.

From the moment we landed in the country, however, it was impossible to ignore the divisions still present. My kids were the first to pick up on it. We were on a hop-on, hop-off bus tour in Johannesburg, driving through a particularly affluent area, when Ayana, wide-eyed, looked at me and asked, "Are those hotels or houses?" I chuckled at her surprise, but the truth of it was inescapable. The homes we were looking at were massive and practically palatial, and nearly all belonged to wealthy White families. Even Ayana, at her age, could sense something was off. The economic gap in South Africa is stark, with most White families enjoying vast wealth while the majority of the Black population continues to live in poverty. It was a sobering realization that even children could see.

Despite progress, economic and social integration continue to lag behind, and the racial divide, though less overt, was palpable. Kasia, not one to miss a detail, added that nearly all the wait staff were Black, serving patrons who were mostly White. It was another clear reminder that while apartheid may have officially ended decades ago, the remnants of that era linger, deeply ingrained in the country's social fabric.

When situations like this arise, I grapple with what to say. We were there to show the girls the beauty and diversity of the world, yet sometimes, the world reveals its difficult truths in ways that are tough to explain. I felt a responsibility not only to acknowledge what they were seeing but also to help them understand that these challenges are not unique to South Africa. As we sat together, I gently reminded them that every country, even our own home in Canada, has its own journey of reckoning with its past and adjusting to the realities of inequality and systemic injustice.

It was a delicate balance—on one hand, teaching them to be aware of the complexities of race and power in the world, and on the other, encouraging them to approach these issues with empathy rather than judgement.

I wanted them to see that progress is not linear, and while it's easy to feel discouraged by what we were witnessing, it's also important to recognize the ongoing efforts of those working tirelessly to heal these wounds. We talked about how change takes time and that learning about these divides is the first step toward becoming part of the solution wherever they find themselves.

Our awareness of this divide only deepened as the trip went on. One day, while we were having lunch, Ayana pointed out that none of the Black and White patrons in the restaurants we visited seemed to sit together. I glanced around and realized she was right. I chalked it up to being an anomaly, but sure enough, it was a recurring theme throughout our stay.

This is something I struggle with as a Dad. It's this ability to walk this tightrope between opening their eyes to the reality of the world while not crushing their spirit. But here's what I keep coming back to—maybe I just need to stop pretending I've got this all figured out. Maybe it's enough to just sit there with them in that uncomfortable space of 'yeah kids, this is really hard, and I wish I had better answers for you.' Because that's the real stuff I'm teaching them, right? Not just about South Africa and its complicated story, but about being a person in this wild world—about staying open when everything in you wants to shut down. I guess it's more like trying to herd cats. Or learning to dance in the dark. Kind of messy. Kind of chaotic. But perhaps worth every stumbling step.

Much of South Africa's history is intertwined with their first democratically elected president, Nelson Mandela. I still remember his release from prison on my birthday that year, February 11, 1990. At the time, I was annoyed he was overshadowing my special day—typical teenager stuff. My parents, annoyed with me, quickly turned it into a history lesson. Funnily enough, a couple of years later, I had the opportunity to meet both Mandela and then-Canadian Prime Minister Brian Mulroney in person when he came to Canada. I've been fascinated by Mandela's life and legacy ever since.

From our apartment in Cape Town, we look out over the beach and the waves of the Atlantic Ocean. In the distance, we can see Robben Island, once home to political prisoners, those with leprosy, and other dissidents. Visiting the island was a somber experience. For 18 of his 27 years in prison, Madiba as Mandela is traditionally referred to, was held here. Our guide on the island, a former political prisoner, returned to provide tours and ensure that future generations heard their stories firsthand. The conditions were harsh, with treatment varying based on how dark your skin colour was. Black prisoners were even given a daily drink to ensure sterility when they were released from jail. Walking through the island's austere buildings and barren grounds, you could almost hear the whispers of its painful past. The most moving part was seeing Mandela's tiny cell and imagining the years he spent confined within those walls. The tour guide's personal anecdotes added a powerful, human touch to the historical facts.

Yet, our trip wasn't all heavy moments of reflection. In fact, one of the most heartwarming experiences we had was visiting a school just outside of a town called Hoedspruit in the northeastern corner of the country. We had arranged to visit a local classroom, and both Ayana and Kasia were excited about meeting the students. When we arrived, the kids were just as thrilled to meet us. They peppered Ayana and Kasia with questions, and our girls did the same in return. There was an instant connection, a blend of curiosity and admiration.

At one point, a few of the students shyly asked if they could trade places with our girls, and I could see the realization dawn on Ayana and Kasia—how fortunate they were to be travelling the world. Our daughters, who had spent the trip processing the inequalities they observed, now found themselves on the other side of privilege. It was one of those rare moments when you can see the impact of an experience on your kids in real time. They were beginning to understand that the opportunities they had were not universal, and I had hoped that this realization would stay with them long after we left.

Some of the students were particularly curious about Canada and its infamous cold winters. None of them had ever seen snow, and Ayana and Kasia, ever the storytellers, launched into vivid descriptions of Canadian winters and their own school environment. The South African students were wide-eyed, listening with a mix of awe and disbelief. It was an apparent contrast to their reality, where temperatures rarely dip below freezing.

While grappling with the complex realities of South African society, we also found moments of pure joy and wonder in the country's natural beauty. No trip to South Africa would be complete without a safari. From the moment we set out into the bush, the adventure took on a magical quality. Within the first 24 hours, we managed to spot the entire Big Five—lion, leopard, cheetah, rhino, and buffalo. I couldn't believe our luck. It was almost as if the animals had all agreed to make an appearance just for us. Meanwhile, a French family we met at the lodge was visibly frustrated. They had been on multiple safaris over several years without even coming close to seeing all the animals. Their envy was palpable, though they tried their best to hide it!

On our safari, we noticed a common dynamic at many high-end lodges: Black drivers with White guides in charge of pointing out the animals. It felt strange, a lingering vestige of the old South Africa that still lingered in the air. But our lodge was different. We had one guide, KK, a Black South African, and he did everything— driving, spotting, and narrating. One evening, as the sun disappeared and darkness blanketed the savannah, KK showed us just how skilled he was. Navigating the pitch-black bush in a manual transmission vehicle, he used a flashlight to search the landscape as we bounced along when suddenly, he brought the vehicle to an abrupt halt. With military precision, he pointed out a tiny chameleon perched on a branch, camouflaged against the night. It was a moment of pure awe. How he managed to spot that tiny creature in the darkness was beyond me. We were convinced KK had some kind of night vision superpower. To this day, I don't know how he did it, but that moment was one of the many instances that made our safari remarkable.

Back at the lodge, the magic of the South African wilderness continued. Every morning on the way to breakfast, we had to tiptoe around a herd of elephants that came to drink water by the pool. These towering creatures would stand just a few feet away, their trunks lazily sloshing water as they stared at us, seemingly unfazed by our presence. It was a surreal experience, to say the least, and one that quickly became part of our routine. There was something profoundly humbling about being so close to such majestic animals in their natural habitat, watching them as they watched us.

Our adventure didn't end in the bush. One of the most memorable parts of our trip was visiting Table Mountain, which is 3,500 ft above sea level in Cape Town. The glass-encased cable car ride to the top was exhilarating, taking about five minutes and continually rotating a full 360 degrees so that every passenger could take in the stunning panoramic views. From the summit, the sight was beyond words—the blue of the Indian and Atlantic Oceans blending with the rugged beauty of Cape Town's coastline. It felt like standing on the edge of the world, the city sprawling below us, the ocean stretching out into the horizon. We spent hours at the top, mesmerized by the sheer beauty of it all, soaking in the crisp air and the overwhelming sense of calm.

South Africa, however, isn't all about dramatic landscapes and wildlife. Sometimes, the most unexpected moments can bring the most joy—and laughter. One of these moments happened in, of all places, a South African pharmacy. We were casually browsing the aisles, picking up a few essentials—sunscreen, some toiletries, the usual—when something on the shelf stopped me in my tracks. I glanced at the display, then did a double take. There, nestled among the men's grooming products, was a package with my face on it.

At first, I thought I was imagining things. I blinked, rubbed my eyes, and leaned in closer to confirm what I was seeing. But no, it was unmistakable—my face, staring back at me from a box of men's shaving products in a pharmacy halfway across the globe. It felt surreal, a peculiar reminder of how one moment in my life could lead to such unexpected outcomes.

I froze, completely dumbfounded, before bursting into a fit of laughter that filled the quiet aisle. The sound must have carried because heads turned in my direction, curious about what could possibly be so funny in the shaving aisle. A man browsing nearby looked over, confused at first, then intrigued. He glanced at the package in my hand, then back at me, his eyes narrowing in recognition. With a puzzled expression, he leaned over and asked, "Are you famous or something?"

I was still laughing when I shook my head, but before I could explain, he blurted out, "Do you know Kanye West?" That question nearly floored me.

Kanye West? Really?

Of all the possibilities, the man's mind jumped straight to Kanye. The randomness of it all made the situation even more surreal. I couldn't help but play along, still laughing at the absurdity of this bizarre brush with 'celebrity.' Several years ago, I had done some modelling work in Vancouver, and as a result, my face now appears on random products all over the world. It was such a long time ago that I have moved on and forgotten. Clearly, these companies know a handsome face when they see it.

Seeing my amusement, the man was now fully convinced he was in the presence of someone famous, or at least someone with a connection to the world of fame. "You know what?" he said, his voice conspiratorial, "You should come golfing with me sometime. I bet we'd have a good laugh." I politely declined his generous offer but couldn't help but appreciate the hilarity of the moment. How could I resist the chance to bring home a piece of South Africa with my face on it? When I showed it to Janice and the girls, they doubled over with laughter, unable to believe the ridiculousness of the situation.

Deep beneath the Earth's surface, in Africa's largest cave system, the ancient Cango Caves hold secrets that span 20 million years. As our group stood in one of its large spaces our guide casually asked if anyone wanted to test the cave's famous acoustics.

You know that moment when someone asks for volunteers and suddenly everyone becomes intensely fascinated with their shoes? That's exactly what happened. But then, breaking through the awkward silence, an English tourist in our group did something unexpected—she turned to our guide and suggested that she should sing instead.

What happened next still gives me goosebumps. After some gentle coaxing, our guide took a deep breath and began to sing 'Ave Maria.' The transformation was instant and magical. I remember my chest tightening as her voice—this incredible, crystal-clear voice I never knew she had—filled the space around us. The acoustics amplified every perfect note until it felt like we were floating in pure sound. I glanced around at my fellow tourists and saw tears streaming down faces, mouths open in awe.

None of us moved.

None of us wanted to break whatever spell had fallen over this space. We just stood there, lost in a moment that felt almost spiritual.

When the final note faded into the darkness, the silence felt electric. I had to know if this was planned—it seemed too perfect not to be. I caught up with the English tourist who'd made the suggestion, my heart still racing. Her response left me even more amazed: "Honestly, it was completely spontaneous—I never expected her to actually do it!"

Sometimes the most extraordinary moments come when you least expect them, like finding an impromptu opera performance in a prehistoric cave. To this day, whenever I hear "Ave Maria," my throat tightens and I'm instantly transported back to that moment, standing in the dark, surrounded by ancient stone, witnessing pure magic emerge from the most unexpected place.

Key Takeaways

1. Acknowledge History: Understanding a country's history is crucial to grasping its present social dynamics and inequalities.

2. Value of Local Voices: Engaging with local guides and community members provides authentic insights into the country's culture and challenges, enhancing the travel experience.

Key Questions

1. How do I confront and learn from the difficult histories of the places I visit?

2. How do my travel experiences shape my understanding of privilege and opportunity?

3. How can I encourage open discussions about race and inequality with my family or peers?

PAUSE & REFLECT: Expanding Your Worldview

1. Examine Inherited Stories

    TODAY: Notice where your preconceptions come from and question one of them

    THIS WEEK: Have an honest conversation with a young person about something difficult you observe

    THIS MONTH: Research the history of your own community's social dynamics

2. Take Conscious Action

    •   Start a small project or initiative that brings people together around a shared goal

    •   Join a group or club that focuses on an interest you've never explored

3. Build Bridges

    •   Partner with someone on a creative or professional project that challenges your usual way of thinking.

    •   Post a reflection online about a new perspective you've gained and how it's shifted your thinking.

A view so grand from Cape of Good Hope, it's hard to believe it's real.

Casting the flavors of Soweto, one snack at a time.

Enjoying breathtaking sights from the summit—nature's masterpiece.

Finally making time to reflect and recharge.

Exploring nature's underground masterpiece.

Endless possibilities - where the land meets the sea.

It took a second to register... but yes, that's me on that product!

Riding the waves of sand like a pro!

Staring into the soul of the wild.

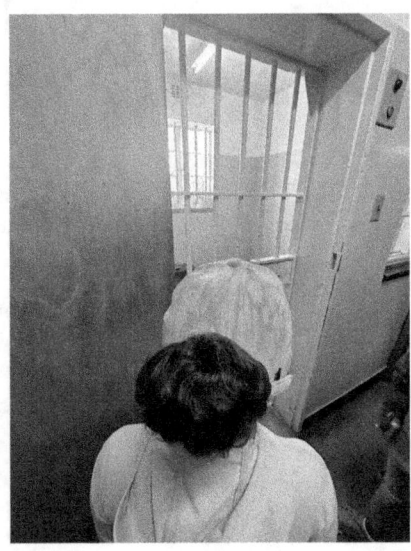

Staring into the walls that held
a man who changed the world.

Step by step, earning those
panoramic views.

The ultimate reminder: we're in
their backyard.

Transforming simple grains into sustenance, one pound at a time.

Turns out, you can't outmuscle Mother Nature.

Waking up to the endless beauty of the Atlantic Ocean— Cape Town, you've captured our heart.

Walking on the edge, where the world feels endles.

When in South Africa, play to the beat of your own drum.

CHAPTER #10
JORDAN

"Sometimes poverty of resources leads
to richness of spirit."
- Paulo Coelho

This trip revealed a truth I've often found in travel: places that are thought to be the most dangerous can, in some cases, be overblown, and regions considered impoverished are often the most hospitable.

Over 20 years ago, I visited the Gulf region for the first time, spending several weeks in Dubai before it gradually transformed into the powerhouse it is today. I assumed most countries in the region were fairly wealthy, given they held some of the world's largest oil deposits and reserves. However, we learned that Jordan, has virtually no oil and relies on imports from neighbouring countries. It also faces significant resource challenges—especially with water, as much of the country is an arid Arabian desert.

Even without this context, Jordan was not high on my list of places to visit. Janice was keen on visiting, but aside from floating in the Dead Sea, I didn't have much interest or know a lot about the country. I've always had a soft spot for unexpected surprises, and Jordan quickly became a delightful revelation as our visit unfolded.

What Jordan lacks in resources, it makes up for in the generosity of its people. Whether we were wandering the chaotic streets of Amman or venturing into the vast deserts of Wadi Rum, the constant offers of tea were more than just courtesy—they showed me that even in a land where the sun bakes the earth until it cracks, the simplest act of sharing can make you feel at home.

Amman, the capital of Jordan, may not be the most visually striking city at first glance. The streets are a bit chaotic, and the summer heat is absolutely relentless. However, no matter where we were going, tea was the universal conversation starter, a symbol of the deep-seated hospitality and kindness that defines the Jordanian people. It is one of the reasons I slowly became so infatuated with the country.

One of the most striking insights about Jordan is its diverse population. Many residents are not originally Jordanian but have come from neighbouring countries such as Iraq, Syria, and Egypt, seeking safety and opportunities to build a better future for their families. In conversations over tea with locals, I was deeply moved by their openness and the spirit of coexistence. Rather than encountering tension or division, there is a remarkable atmosphere of acceptance and shared resilience.

As we wandered the streets of Amman, it became clear that the culinary culture was as rich as its people. Every meal became an opportunity to experience not just the flavours of Jordan but the stories behind each dish.

In fact our Jordanian food tour was meant to be a three-hour culinary journey, but it quickly turned into a six-hour marathon of eating and drinking as we dove deep into the vibrant markets of Amman. The tantalizing aromas from each food stall pulled us in, offering irresistible bites that told the story of Jordan's rich heritage. From the crispy, golden falafel to the creamy, yogurt-laden mansaf and the decadent sweetness of knafeh (pronounced que-nah-feh), every dish seemed better than the last.

Our guide, Jumana, who had the kind of local clout that made it seem like she was the defacto mayor, took us from one vendor to the next, weaving in stories about Amman's history and its people. Her energy was infectious, and her connections meant that at every stop, we were greeted with open arms and—of course—more food. We were full, happy, and a little wiser about the importance of food in Jordanian culture.

While the warmth of Jordan's people and the richness of its culture had won us over, there was one challenge we couldn't escape—quite literally. Jordan's deep-rooted tobacco culture permeated every aspect of daily life. While most countries have clamped down hard on smoking, Jordan seemed to embrace it with open arms. Whether it was cigarettes, shisha, or cigars, smoking wasn't just common—it was in their DNA. The country has one of the highest rates of smoking by adults anywhere in the world

We were surrounded by cigarette smoke everywhere. From airports to restaurants and even department stores, smoking was simply a part of the daily rhythm. I couldn't remember the last time I was asked, "Would you prefer a smoking or non-smoking room?" in a hotel—until Jordan. The redundancy of that question really hit me when we walked into a restaurant labelled as having a 'non-smoking section.' In reality, it was just one large room with non-smokers (just us) huddled awkwardly at one end while everyone else on the other side happily puffed away. The smoke clearly didn't get the memo about staying in its section.

A cough I picked up in the country lingered the entire trip, a stubborn souvenir from all the secondhand smoke we inhaled. It felt like no matter where we went, there was no escape from the haze. Despite Jordan's many charms, the omnipresent smoke was literally in the air we breathed.

When the unrest unfolded in the Middle East in October 2023, tourism to Jordan dropped like a stone in a bucket. Despite being a stable country, it was as if someone had flipped the 'off' switch on international travel to this captivating destination.

When we arrived in early July, the impact was still very evident. Sometimes it felt like we had to remind locals to turn the lights back on—we were here and eager to explore what the country had to offer. In one sense, it was surreal, almost as if we were seeing a side of Jordan that few people would ever get to experience: the calm after the storm. Popular tourist hotspots like the Dead Sea, Petra, and Aqaba, which are normally flooded with camera-toting travellers, felt eerily quiet. The legendary sites that typically attract hordes of tourists were practically deserted. We had them almost entirely to ourselves—a strange privilege offering us rare, intimate encounters with history and nature.

And speaking of history, we were completely caught off guard by the sheer number of Roman ruins scattered across Jordan. I mean, when you think 'Romans,' your mind probably wanders to Italy, maybe Greece— not the middle of the Arabian desert. Yet here they were, these magnificent remnants of the Roman Empire, looking somewhat out of place but absolutely spectacular. The Romans, it turns out, were basically the ancient world's most ambitious real estate developers, building cities wherever they went. Jordan has some of the best preserved Roman ruins outside of Italy, complete with grand colonnaded streets, theatres, and temples that would make Caesar proud. It's as if the Romans looked at this harsh desert landscape and thought, 'You know what this place needs? Some fancy marble columns and an amphitheatre.'

This unusual emptiness at historical sites had an unexpected silver lining—the incredible warmth and hospitality we experienced. The graciousness with which we were welcomed felt like something reserved for royalty. At times, it was even a little embarrassing, like when you're being treated to something that feels too good to be true, and you can't help but wonder, 'What's the catch?' Initially, we were concerned, thinking we might be taken advantage of, but that feeling didn't last long.

The same trust and generosity that initially made us feel cautious quickly became one of the highlights of our trip. After spending the day exploring the stunning ruins of Petra, we were exhausted and couldn't wait to sit down for a hearty meal. We stumbled upon a small local restaurant, the kind that promised authentic Jordanian flavours and an escape from the midday heat. As we tucked into our plates of freshly made hummus, warm bread, and tender grilled meats, the meal felt like the perfect end to our Petra adventure. But just as we were finishing up, we noticed something—total silence. The bustling sounds of the town had faded, and the restaurant was nearly empty except for us.

It quickly dawned on us that it was Friday afternoon, and in a predominantly Muslim country, this meant one thing—Friday prayers. The entire town had made its way to the mosque, leaving us the last diners standing. The owner and waitstaff approached our table with smiles and a bit of urgency, politely informing us they were all heading out for prayers. Then, with a casual wave toward the kitchen, the owner said something I've never heard in my life: "If you need anything, help yourself. Just lock the door on your way out."

We all exchanged wide-eyed looks, trying to process what the owner just said. Kasia laughed, saying, "This would never happen at home!" And she was right. I mean, imagine a restaurant back home just handing you the keys and saying, 'Help yourself, we trust you!' We chuckled at the thought of us suddenly running a Jordanian restaurant for the next hour. They had placed their faith in us, complete strangers, to finish our meal and help ourselves if necessary.

As they left, we found ourselves alone, sipping our drinks and soaking in the absurdity of the situation. We were tempted to poke around in the kitchen just for the novelty of it, but ultimately, we paid our bill and closed the door behind us, still laughing at how this little slice of life could be so wonderfully different from anything we'd ever experienced before. It was such a refreshingly laid-back and trusting approach—one that made us love Jordan all the more.

If anything, what I learned from that experience is that sometimes the deepest trust isn't found in grand gestures, but in the casual confidence of a restaurant owner who hands you the keys to their livelihood without a second thought. In those quiet moments when we sat alone in that empty restaurant, we weren't just witnessing Jordanian hospitality — we were learning that sometimes the most profound connections happen when someone chooses to see you as trustworthy, even before you've earned it. Sure, a cynic might point out that Jordan's strict social codes help make such trust possible, but in a world where genuine faith in strangers seems to grow rarer by the day, there was something quietly revolutionary about that simple gesture. That's the thing about trust: when someone offers it freely, it has a way of making you want to be worthy of it.

When you travel, you want authenticity. You want to live like the locals or at least understand what it's like to live like them in their environment. Some opt for this with a touch of 'Western comfort' too. Our experience with the Bedouins, once a nomadic Arab tribe, was nothing like this. We were greeted in a parking lot, entering the town of Wadi Rum, by Mohammed in his beat-up 4x4 Toyota pickup truck. For whatever reason, the 4x4 Toyota pick-up truck seems to be the vehicle du jour in Jordan. We took a bumpy and lengthy drive into the Arabian desert. We dropped our stuff off and proceeded to take our camels the rest of the way.

I have never ridden a horse, let alone a camel, and what an experience this was. What people don't tell you is that you should clearly stretch before getting onto a camel. Or risk walking like a cowboy who lost his horse for the rest of the day. These animals are beautiful and astounding. Their humps can store up to 80 lbs (35 kg) of fat, which they can live off for weeks and even months. Camels may have their humps, but after our food tour in Amman, I was carrying my own little 'travel pouch' around my waist. We made a brief stop to enjoy a snack and as I dismounted my camel, I made the mistake of letting go of its harness, forgetting to hang on to it. In Jordan, they say, 'Pray to Allah, but tie your camel.' I almost learned the truth the hard way. Camels, as our guide Abdel explained, can run at speeds of almost 60 km/hr (40 miles/hr) and would have left me stranded in no time. Thankfully, Abdel acted quickly, skillfully grabbing the harness just before it hit the ground, saving me from what could have been a very long walk back to base camp.

The vast expanse of Wadi Rum stretched endlessly before us, its scorched landscape shimmering under the unforgiving summer sun, with temperatures frequently climbing to 40°C (100°F). Even as night fell, the heat lingered, never fully retreating. Our three–day stay with the Bedouins in this iconic Arabian desert was one of the most striking chapters of our journey. Their nomadic heritage, boundless hospitality, and profound knowledge of the desert left a lasting impression.

When we arrived for dinner, it felt like we'd stepped into a scene straight from a movie. A crackling fire cast flickering shadows, while vibrant rugs lay carefully spread around it, inviting us to sit and enjoy the warmth. Generous servings of Jordanian coffee and tea circulated, filling the air with comforting, spiced aromas. Yet, one thing was conspicuously missing: the food. Curious, I politely asked Mohammed when dinner would be ready. He smiled knowingly and pointed down to the ground. My puzzled expression only made his grin widen.

What he revealed was zarb, a cherished Bedouin cooking tradition that transforms a simple meal into an unforgettable experience. Imagine this: marinated meat and seasoned vegetables are wrapped and then buried in a hand-dug oven several feet beneath the sandy earth. The oven, lined with hot coals, cradles the food as it's sealed with a heavy metal lid and buried under sand to capture every bit of heat. Over hours, the ingredients gently roast in their own juices, with the desert's warmth turning the meat tender and succulent, while the vegetables absorb a rich, smoky essence.

Finally, when unearthed, the mouthwatering aromas are undeniable—each bite carries the taste of the desert itself: deeply flavorful, soft, and steeped in tradition.

We stayed for two nights, nestled in a cave, surrounded by the vast beauty of the desert, a landscape that felt as ancient as time itself. The sky above us glittered with countless stars, making us feel as if we were part of something timeless. Mohammed enriched our stay with stories of ancient desert lore, sharing tales of treasure hunts that sounded straight out of an Indiana Jones adventure. He took a special interest in our girls, teaching them the rules of Bedouin chess, a game with centuries of history. By the flickering firelight, they eagerly learned the game's strategies and showed off their quick understanding, playing match after match with Mohammed. The following evening, they had the chance to test their newfound chess skills with another family visiting from Tokyo and staying in a nearby cave. This unique blend of cultural immersion, adventure, and comfort made our nights in Wadi Rum feel like we were stepping into a living storybook.

Before going to bed, we looked up to see the night sky come alive—shooting stars streaked across the heavens, the Milky Way shimmered, and the planets revealed themselves untouched by light pollution.

Kasia remarked that it felt like an IMAX theatre, but this was no simulation—it was the raw beauty of the universe in its most authentic form.

The ancient stillness of Wadi Rum enveloped us, and in that moment, it became clear: there are very few places left like this in the world. It felt as if we had been transported back thousands of years to a time that had remained nearly unchanged. The vastness of the desert made me acutely aware of how small we are on this planet. It was humbling, to say the least.

Despite the overwhelming sense of peace around us, sleep didn't come easily on that first night in the outdoor cave. Part of it was the sheer awe of the starry spectacle overhead, and part of it was an ever—present awareness of the nocturnal creatures in the desert, quietly prowling in search of their next meal.

It was in those moments when we were lying awake halfway between awe and unease that everything felt surreal. Here we were, sophisticated enough to name constellations and track shooting stars using our cellphones, but still jumping at every little sound in the darkness—just like our ancestors must have done thousands of years ago. And maybe that's what makes places like Wadi Rum so special. For a brief moment, you get to be both: the modern stargazer and the ancient human whose heart still skips a beat at a desert wolf's howl. I guess we haven't changed as much as we like to think.

One of Jordan's sheer surprises was the number of sandstorms that swept through the desert. These mini hurricanes were quick and fierce. Sand, dust, garbage, and the odd plastic bag were swept up in a matter of seconds, and then, just like that, it was over. It was unreal. The terrain of the Arabian desert in Jordan has this dusty, red soil that mimics the images of what we have seen on Mars. In fact, many movies utilize scenes from here to reflect that extraterrestrial environment.

Travelling through the Middle East, you can't help but be astounded by the sheer number of biblical locations located in this region. Witnessing the site of Jesus' baptism in the River Jordan by John the Baptist or standing on the mountaintop of Mt. Nebo, where Moses showed the Israelites the Promised Land, is astounding. Even for the non-religious, it is a sight to behold.

While the historical and biblical significance of Jordan is undeniable, we soon discovered that its people have a strong cultural emphasis on family, and our own small family became quite the conversation starter. Jordan has a deep infatuation with big families. Many people we came across on the trip were dumbfounded that we only had two kids. At one point, an elderly Jordanian man pulled me aside to ask again, just in case I was shy about admitting to any children I might have had outside of marriage. Pretty bold, right? The dynamics of having two daughters also weighed heavily on many Jordanians. The fact that I did not have a son was a bit of a disappointment, and I was strongly encouraged to follow the maxim—'if at first you don't succeed, try and try again.' One particularly determined elder even suggested I drink more camel's milk, assuring me that it would guarantee a son. Janice was not amused, and I emphasized my happiness with my two angels—quite content to keep things as they were despite numerous attempts to convince me otherwise over tea or camel's milk.

In retrospect, my initial indifference towards Jordan feels laughable. With its dusty streets, overwhelming heat, and lingering tobacco scent, this country managed to capture my heart in ways I never expected. Jordan's charm lies not in its aesthetics but in its people and their stories, the unexpected kindness of strangers, and the profound historical and cultural experiences that sneak up on you when you least expect them.

If travel is about discovering the soul of a place, then Jordan, with all its quirks and wonders, is a soulful masterpiece.

Key Takeaways

1. Challenge Your Assumptions: Don't write off destinations based on preconceptions — the places you expect least from often surprise you the most.

2. True Wealth Isn't Material: A country's richness isn't measured by its resources but by its people's generosity and spirit.

3. Trust Breeds Trust: When someone extends trust freely—like a restaurant owner handing over their keys—it makes you want to be worthy of that trust.

Key Questions

1. What assumptions do I hold about people or places that I have never visited, and how might I challenge those beliefs?

2. In what ways can I find beauty and value in experiences that initially seem uncomfortable or different from my norm?

PAUSE & REFLECT: Trust and Transformation

1. Open Your Mind

    TODAY: List three non-material riches in your life

    THIS WEEK: Experience something that costs nothing but creates lasting memories

    THIS MONTH: Visit a place known for simplicity rather than luxury

2. Practice Radical Trust

    • Accept an unexpected invitation

    • Let someone else plan an outing or experience for you without knowing the details

    • Let go of one preconception you hold about a place or people

3. Cultivate Hospitality

    • Share what you have, however modest it might seem

    • Find ways to make strangers feel like family

A feast of falafels, crispy on the outside and perfectly savory inside.

A perfect plate of
Mediterranean delights.

A sea of olives at the market in
Amman – the colors are just as
delicious as they look.

Awake to a new day in the quiet of the desert cave.

Following the path to Petra for the first time – a magical adventure begins.

Just having a deep conversation with a camel. Turns out we have a lot in common.

Relaxing with a view – enjoying the sunset at the Dead Sea.

Stepping back in time to take in the breathtaking view of a Roman amphitheatre below.

This Roman hallway captures history in every glow in Jordan.

Walking in the footsteps of history through Petra.

CHAPTER #11
REFLECTIONS AND
REVELATIONS

"Family is the compass that guides us; travel is the journey
that helps us rediscover our true selves."
– Anonymous

When we first set out on this journey, I was bracing
myself for the inevitable family tension that would
come from constant togetherness. After all, who
wouldn't get tired of their family after weeks of non-stop
interaction? But amid the occasional eye-rolling and
snippy comments, I discovered something unexpected:
we genuinely enjoyed each other's company. Sure, there
were times when everyone's patience wore thin, but
those fleeting moments of irritation were overshadowed
by a deeper sense of connection that began to shape
our journey in ways I never anticipated.

Like any grand adventure, we quickly learned that expectations rarely match reality. This became especially apparent during our long car rides—an ironic twist for a family that proudly lived 'car-free' in Toronto. My romantic visions of cross-country driving lost their shine somewhere between mediating armrest backseat territory wars and maintaining a steady supply of snacks to ward off hangry meltdowns. Yet these moments of chaos led us to one of our most valuable discoveries: the art of dividing and conquering.

We realized we didn't need to move as a pack of four all the time. Those precious one-on-one moments with each daughter became transformative. Whether it was exploring a market with Kasia or taking Ayana for a morning swim, these solo adventures created space for real conversations and connection. Without their sister around, each girl opened up differently, sharing thoughts and stories they might have kept to themselves in the group. The best part? At dinner, we'd all catch up, sharing our individual adventures with genuine interest and excitement. These separate experiences actually brought us closer together, giving us fresh stories to tell and new perspectives to share.

Out of necessity, we found ourselves limiting iPhone screen time during our longer travels. At first, our kids acted like we'd removed their vital organs—there was moaning, dramatic sighs, and claims of impending death by boredom. But then, in those empty spaces where constant scrolling used to live, something magical happened.

Creativity bloomed.

Made-up games materialized from nowhere, epic stories were crafted, and yes, sometimes they just gazed out the car window, lost in thought or making up stories about the landscapes we passed.

The surprising twist?

Without the constant stream of Netflix shows or movies, they seemed more centered, more present. In embracing boredom, they'd stumbled upon something valuable—the art of entertaining themselves with nothing but their imaginations and the world around them.

Those quiet moments of creativity and connection didn't mean our journey was all smooth sailing. Travel has a way of testing you, and we had our fair share of mishaps that tested our collective patience. Take our adventure in Petra, for instance. Picture this: We're dripping with sweat, our legs burning from a hike that's pushed us way beyond our comfort zone. What we thought would be a breezy 3-hour walk turned into an epic trek through searing heat when we took one wrong turn. While other tourists hopped on donkeys to escape the sun, we stubbornly pressed on, determined to finish what we'd started—though looking less like intrepid explorers and more like a sweaty, sand-covered group of misfits.

A year ago, this kind of miscalculation would have crushed our spirits. But something fascinating happened to us on the trek. We'd learned to embrace our failures, even find joy in them. The idea is simple—the more mistakes or missteps you experience, the less they embarrass or deter you. I started calling it our 'failure immunity'—like a superpower that grew stronger with each mishap. The beauty wasn't just in how we handled the big setbacks, but in watching each of us evolve from anxious perfectionists into resilient adventurers who could laugh at their mistakes. (Well, mostly—we're still not quite ready to chuckle about that particular day in Petra's heat!)

Travel didn't just change our children—it transformed how we approached parenting altogether. Back home, I often found myself operating on autopilot: solving problems quickly, steering clear of risks, maintaining routines at all costs. But being in constantly changing environments forced me to parent differently. I learned to step back, allowing my children to navigate unfamiliar situations on their own terms.

This newfound resilience showed up differently in each of us. Ayana's transformation in the water was nothing short of miraculous. Just a year ago, she had a near-drowning incident at a friend's pool, and now she's fearlessly leaping into the ocean without a second thought. With very few swimming lessons under her belt, it's just pure joy and a love for the water. Watching her swim in Albania's turquoise sea, it hit me how resilient kids are. They have a way of surprising you when you least expect it, reminding you that sometimes, all they need is a little space to figure things out on their own.

While Ayana conquered her fears in the water, her sister Kasia was busy showing her own kind of quiet strength. While some kids might bluntly point out that Dad's been enjoying too many food tours, Kasia has her own subtle way. I discovered my increasingly snug shorts had been mysteriously altered one morning—secretly fixed by my daughter who, apparently, had picked up sewing skills when I wasn't looking. When I thanked her, she just gave me that classic Kasia look—one eyebrow slightly raised—and said with perfect deadpan delivery, "Just looking out for you, Daddy." That's Kasia in a nutshell: observant, thoughtful, and always one step ahead, with just enough dry humor to keep me humble.

Behind all these individual transformations was Janice's extraordinary strength and vision. This whole adventure began with her dream, her unwavering belief that we could pull off something this ambitious. While I often found myself overwhelmed by the complexity of it all, sometimes wondering if we should just call it off, her quiet confidence never wavered. Her attention to detail and tenacity turned what seemed impossible into our reality. She had this remarkable gift for anticipating problems before they arose, making the difficult seem effortless, and keeping us all moving forward even when doubts crept in. Our trip wouldn't have been possible without her steady hand guiding us through every step.

Her preparation reminded me how important it is to lead by example. Janice didn't just tell our daughters to be resilient or adaptable—she modeled it. When things went awry, she showed calm in chaos and persistence in uncertainty. Her ability to find solutions on the fly didn't just reassure me; it inspired me. Watching her lead, I realized how much our daughters were absorbing from her every day—not through lectures, but through her actions.

For me, there was a particular freedom in not being tethered to how others previously defined me. Meeting new people along the way, I relished the opportunity to simply be seen as I was in that moment—not as a manager, a neighbour, or any of the other roles I played back home. In these fresh interactions, I could just exist without the weight of assumptions or expectations. It's a strange and wonderful feeling to realize that your past doesn't always need to follow you.

Navigating the world as a biracial family added another layer to our journey. Before this trip, I'll admit I was curious—and if I'm honest, a bit nervous about how we'd be perceived. In South Africa, where the shadow of apartheid still looms, I found myself hyper-aware of the glances directed our way. Curiously, when I asked people throughout our journey where they thought we were from, most shrugged and confidently declared that we must be diplomats, expats, or Americans from Chicago. This became a running joke among us; every time we approached locals to ask where they thought we hailed from, without fail, they would say, "Chicago!" I'm still unclear on exactly what that means. Do we have a 'Chicago vibe' I'm unaware of?

In Albania, we were often the only mixed-race family around, and the stares we got were less about judgment and more about sheer curiosity. At first, it was unsettling. I worried about how the girls might feel, whether they'd internalize that sense of being different in a negative way. But as the days passed, I realized the stares didn't carry malice; they carried intrigue. And the more I relaxed, the more I saw it as an opportunity to show people that families like ours are just as natural as any other, no matter what we look like.

Kasia, for her part, was unbothered. She took every assumption in stride, especially when people mistakenly thought we were from the U.S. With a proud smile and that confidence only she can muster, she'd correct them: "We're Canadian!" (That's a very important distinction for her.) Watching her stand firm in her identity, I couldn't help but feel a swell of pride. It was a reminder that, for all my overthinking, my daughters are growing up in a world where they can confidently claim who they are, no matter where they are.

Looking back on this journey now, I find myself struck by how much we've all grown. Not just physically (though watching the girls outgrow their carefully packed clothes at an alarming rate was quite something), but in those deeper, more meaningful ways that aren't as easy to measure. The daily rush of life back home often left little room for noticing these subtle transformations. But here, stripped of our usual routines and distractions, every small change became magnified.

For me, I've discovered a new lightness in my step, a deeper sense of gratitude for the simple things. Those long conversations with strangers that once made my daughters roll their eyes have become treasured moments of connection. I'm learning to accept that there are countless things in the external world beyond my control, and surprisingly, I'm okay with that now. The constant need to plan, to worry about what's next, has been replaced by something more valuable—the ability to simply be present.

What strikes me most is how travel has this sneaky way of teaching you things you didn't even know you needed to learn. Like how strength often shows up in the quiet moments—in Ayana's determined treading of water, in Kasia's subtle acts of care, in Janice's unwavering belief in our family's ability to pull this off. Sometimes the best moments aren't the ones you carefully planned but the unexpected ones. Like being trusted with a restaurant's keys during prayer time or watching your kids invent elaborate games in the backseat of a car when there's 'nothing to do.'

Perhaps the most powerful lesson has been about the simple act of pausing. Back home, life moves at such a relentless pace that we forget we have permission to just stop, breathe, and be present. This journey has shown me that these pauses aren't luxuries—they're necessities. They're the moments when you actually see your children growing before your eyes, when you notice the small gestures of love that might otherwise slip by unnoticed, when you feel the full weight of gratitude for this life you're living.

There's something magical that happens when you slow down enough to notice life unfolding around you. After this journey, I don't want to wait for "someday" to find these moments of connection. I want to remember that I can pause right in the middle of a regular Wednesday afternoon back home—to really see my girls growing up before my eyes, to have those random chats with strangers that drive my kids crazy, to just breathe and be present.

The biggest lesson from all of this?

The real adventure isn't in the stamps in our passports, but in those small moments when we're truly present with each other. It's watching your kids become braver, wiser, and funnier than you ever imagined. And sometimes, it's about learning to get out of your own way, to trust that things will work out, and to just enjoy the ride.

Key Takeaways

1. Permission to Pause: Learning to slow down and be present revealed that the real adventures aren't in the destinations, but in noticing the small moments of connection along the way.

2. Cherish Every Phase: Each stage of your children's growth offers its own unique joys and challenges, reminding you to cherish the fleeting moments of childhood.

3. Make Mistakes: Failure immunity is about seeing setbacks as growth opportunities. Embracing mistakes helps us build resilience, adapt, and stay focused on the bigger journey.

Key Questions

1. How do you practice mindfulness and live in the moment while travelling? Reflect on the importance of savouring experiences rather than just checking off destinations.

2. As a parent, how do you balance guiding your children while allowing them the space to grow and explore on their own?

3. How can embracing failure as a learning experience help you stay resilient and motivated in the face of challenges?

PAUSE & REFLECT: Embracing Growth and Connection

1. Cultivate Gratitude

    TODAY: Share a compliment with someone you interact with frequently, expressing genuine appreciation.

    THIS WEEK: Practice a random act of kindness for a neighbour or colleague.

    THIS MONTH: Reflect on a positive experience from the past month and share it with someone close to you.

2. Push Beyond Comfort Zones

    *   Encourage kids to explore a hobby or activity outside their usual interests

    *   View challenges and setbacks as opportunities to develop resilience and adaptability.

3. Cherish Individual Journeys

    *   Make time for one-on-one moments with each child

    *   Allow space for each person's unique growth

    *   Celebrate how your differences enrich your family

CHAPTER #12
ADVENTURES AND
MISADVENTURES

"Travel isn't always pretty. It isn't always comfortable.
Sometimes it hurts, it even breaks your heart. But that's
okay. The journey changes you; it should change you."
– Anthony Bourdain

Before we even left, the idea of a trip around the world
sounded like pure magic to Janice and me. We pictured
endless adventure, cultural immersion, and a lifetime's
worth of stories in every destination. But when we
shared this grand vision with our kids, their reaction
was... well, let's just say less than enthusiastic. Kasia, in
particular, was disappointed. The thought of missing
her elementary school graduation and all the fun that
came with it? In her world, this was nothing short of
catastrophic. She was disgruntled, upset, and downright
devastated.

Cue every adjective for pre-teen angst imaginable.

It wasn't until we were well into the trip that she even started to warm up to the idea. In hindsight, we probably should've involved her in the planning; being the old soul she is, Kasia would've appreciated having a say in the matter. But honestly, who wouldn't be excited about the adventure of a lifetime? Apparently, I'd been projecting my own enthusiasm and completely missed the emotional earthquake that came with pulling a kid away from her social universe.

Ayana, on the other hand, met the news with utter bewilderment. "We are going where? For how long? Why?" She barely glanced up from her Lego, probably thinking we were dragging her on yet another 'exotic vacation,' but this one had the audacity to be longer. Her concerns, however, were surprisingly pragmatic for a 7-year-old. "Are you sure we should be doing this?" "What about school?" and my personal favourite, "Who's going to take care of the house?" These were practical questions we had answers for, but I didn't expect them to come from our youngest. It felt like she'd suddenly become our tiny, reluctant family advisor while I was ready to throw caution to the wind.

Little did we know that our kids' initial reluctance would soon be the least of our travel challenges. While I was busy dreaming about epic adventures and plotting dots on a world map, I completely missed what was epic in their world right then. For Kasia, graduating with her friends — the same kids she'd known since kindergarten — meant everything. And there I was, thinking 'But honey, we're going to snorkel in the Great Barrier Reef!' as if that could somehow replace her moment to shine. Ayana's practical little questions about the house and school were her way of trying to make sense of her whole world shifting. It taught me something I'll never forget: sometimes the biggest adventures in a kid's life aren't the ones that cover the most miles, but the ones that matter most to them.

It's funny how the moment of truth hits you when you realize this is really happening. One minute, you're cozy in Toronto, and many hours later, you're halfway across the globe in an entirely different hemisphere. The ease of modern travel feels like magic—until, of course, the magic decides to take an unexpected vacation of its own.

Now, we had meticulously planned this whole trip. I'm talking spreadsheets with over 30+ flights, each one strategically chosen to minimize headaches. I'd even started feeling a bit smug about how smooth everything had been. No missed flights, no lost luggage, and no one down with food poisoning—how had we pulled this off with almost 90% of the trip complete? But as they say, 'If you want to make the universe laugh, tell it your plans.'

And boy, did the universe have a good chuckle at our expense.

The first sign of trouble came, as it often does, with an overinflated sense of confidence on my part. Our flight from Jordan to Albania had been bombarding my inbox with updates, each seeming more harmless than the last. I'd started treating them like spam—just another digital hiccup, right? So when I tried to check in 24 hours before departure and the system gave me an error, I shrugged it off. That is, until I saw the social media response that made my heart drop into my stomach: "The reason why you cannot check in is that your flight is boarding in 15 minutes." Panic gripped me as I fumbled with my phone, barely able to process the words.

I burst upstairs, where Janice and the kids were lounging blissfully unaware, enjoying their last moments of peace before Hurricane Dad made landfall. Breathless and wild-eyed, I tried to explain the situation, my voice hitting octaves I didn't know I possessed. Janice, my eternal voice of reason, listened patiently, then smiled that calm smile that always makes everything seem manageable. "Let's just find a new flight," she said, as if ordering takeout.

Unfortunately, it was not that simple. It turns out that low-cost carriers are called 'low-cost' for a reason—convenience is not included in the package deal. This policy meant we couldn't book a new flight online so close to departure. No, no, that would be too easy. We had to go to the airport in person. Because, apparently, it's still 1995. So, we spent the afternoon neck-deep in exorbitant fees, frustrating wait times, and logistical nightmares that could've made even a Zen monk lose his cool.

By 3 a.m. the next day, we were back at the airport. The kids, despite the ungodly hour, were surprisingly chipper. Kasia was humming some pop song, and Ayana was quite content to say she was awake before the sun, and there I was, just trying to hold it all together. They were thriving in this 'life on the road' situation, clearly more adaptable than their father.

But of course, smooth sailing isn't part of our travel narrative. We boarded, praying for a peaceful flight, only to have the peace shattered by a young woman sitting ahead of us who seemed to be in an intense dialogue— with herself. At first, I thought maybe she was just really into her pre-flight mantra. But as the plane taxied to the runway, she sprang up, declared, "I need to get off!" and refused to sit down. Flight attendants tried coaxing her back to her seat, but no dice. They ended up turning the plane around, returning to the gate, and escorting her off in what seemed like an overdramatic holiday movie scene.

That wasn't enough drama, because security procedure dictates that when someone disembarks unexpectedly, every single overhead bin must be opened, and every bag in the cargo hold must be matched to its owner. So there we sat, for hours, as bags were shuffled, passengers grumbled, and the kids, in their half-asleep stupor, mumbled, "Are we in Albania yet?"

Not quite, kids. Not quite.

Three hours later, we were finally airborne and made it to Albania, via Istanbul. Touching down in Tirana, I turned to Janice with a rare moment of victory: "Hey, at least our luggage made it." I spoke too soon. Since it was a low-cost airline, we had to check our bags—a rarity on our trip—but it happened. As we stood by the carousel, bag after bag tumbled down before we realized that one bag was left behind in Amman.

There was a silver lining—our car rental attendant, possibly feeling sorry for our bedraggled selves, upgraded us to a shiny new vehicle. I'll admit it lifted my spirits. Thank goodness for small victories, right?

Unfortunately, the Albanian adventure took a detour from there. Shortly after our arrival, the girls were struck down by brutal food poisoning. Apparently, 'travel broadens the mind,' but it can also take a jab at your gut. They spent days confined to bed while Janice, also succumbing to the same cruel bug, binged Netflix like a professional. Forget exploring Albania; she was going to catch up on her favourite shows, even if it killed her.

By the time we left Albania, we were far from defeated, just a little worse for wear. London awaited, and with it, a mini-family reunion and the excitement of the Opening Ceremonies of the Olympic Games across the Channel in Paris. We arrived at our Airbnb in London, eager to put the travel woes behind us, take hot showers, and relax with some nearby takeout. But, of course, this trip had other plans. The door to our apartment wouldn't open. I tried the code, Janice tried the code, heck, even Kasia gave it a shot.

Nothing.

A series of increasingly desperate calls to the owner later, we discovered the Airbnb host had given us the wrong code. Even worse, she was unreachable. So there we stood, stranded on a London sidewalk, luggage in tow, utterly exhausted and out of options. Luckily, with my remaining hotel points, I managed to scrape together a family suite at a last-minute hotel in Central London. Crisis averted.

Despite the parade of mishaps that seemed determined to follow us across continents, something surprising emerged from the chaos—we laughed a lot. These became the stories we would tell, the kind that make you chuckle years later, even if at the time you wanted to curl up in a ball and cry. Each misstep was a testament to the family's resilience and adaptability, and if nothing else, we pulled it off.

So, there we sat in a hotel room in Central London, enjoying an unexpected moment of calm. It hit me then—this, not the picture-perfect shots, not the meticulous itineraries, was the essence of travel. It was in the shared madness, the resilience, the unplanned detours. After all, isn't that where the best stories come from?

Key Takeaways

1. Embrace Flexibility: Expect the unexpected during travel. Stay adaptable, solution-oriented, and positive when faced with inevitable challenges and mishaps.

2. Unscripted Moments: Find meaning in unplanned experiences. Embrace the detours and obstacles as opportunities for family bonding and creating lifelong travel stories.

Key Questions

1. Can you think of a recent experience where humour changed the outcome of a challenging moment?

2. What are some valuable lessons you've learned from difficult travel experiences or family adventures? How have these experiences shaped your understanding of resilience?

PAUSE & REFLECT: Lessons in Adaptability and Resilience

1. Embrace the Unexpected

   TODAY: Reflect on a recent challenge and identify one positive takeaway.

   THIS WEEK: Plan an outing or activity without over-scheduling—leave room for spontaneity and see where it leads.

   THIS MONTH: Celebrate small victories, like finding solutions to unexpected problems or simply laughing through the chaos.

2. Foster Emotional Awareness

   - Discuss how each family member or colleague processes disappointment and excitement differently.

   - Encourage open conversations about feelings, especially when plans change.

   - Acknowledge and validate each family member's unique emotional journey.

3. Deepen Family Connections

   - Reflect on how overcoming challenges together builds resilience and unity.

   - Share stories about past missteps to appreciate the growth and humor that come with them.

CHAPTER #13
THE JOURNEY CONTINUES

"Twenty years from now, you'll be more disappointed by
the things you didn't do than by the ones you did do."
– Mark Twain

Our journey around the world was far more than a
simple escape from the routines of work and daily life;
it was an experience that will forever shape how we see
the world, ourselves, and each other, particularly for my
young kids. What started as a quest to explore faraway
places and immerse ourselves in unfamiliar cultures
became an unintentional journey of self-reflection,
family bonding, and growth.

One of the most profound lessons we learned along
the way was that despite the diversity of languages,
traditions, and cultures, people everywhere share more
similarities than differences. Whether in the remote
village of Pogradec, the bustling streets of Amman, or
the vast expanse of the Hooker Valley, we saw firsthand
that everyone, regardless of where they live, strives for

the same things: building better lives for themselves and their families, finding joy in small moments, and experiencing the world with curiosity. This universal human connection stayed with us throughout our travels, reminding us that no matter how vast the world may seem, we are all deeply connected by our shared dreams.

Our journey also taught us the value of presence over quantity. We made a conscious choice to spend more time in fewer places, understanding that less means more. During our month in Australia, we deliberately stuck to the east coast, diving deep into its wonders rather than spreading ourselves too thinly across the vast continent. This approach allowed us to fully immerse ourselves in each location, truly savouring every experience and encounter. By embracing this slower, more deliberate pace, we found joy in spontaneity, allowing ourselves to be swept away by the unplanned and unexpected — a stark contrast to the meticulously scheduled life we'd left behind.

It was in Australia where I learned to embrace my own spontaneity, even at the cost of my adult dignity. Picture this: like a character from a cartoon floating through the air following a delicious scent, I found myself literally wandering toward beachside barbecues in Cairns, completely hypnotized by the smell of grilling meat –

despite having just eaten lunch. A cheerful Aussie caught me basically drooling near his grill, and instead of being weirded out, he simply grinned and offered me a bite of his masterpiece — a ridiculous pork chop dripping with melted cheese that honestly changed my life for about thirty seconds. The best part? He insisted on giving me the entire pork chop. You should have seen my family's faces: Janice giving me that 'seriously?' look, my pre-teen Kasia dying of embarrassment, and Ayana just cracking up at her Dad acting like a kid who'd just hit the snack jackpot.

That spontaneous moment in Australia, where I let go of my usual reserved demeanour, became an example for the bigger changes ahead. It taught me that sometimes the best opportunities come when we're willing to embrace the unexpected, even if it means looking a bit foolish.

As we transition back to our day-to-day lives, the biggest challenge that keeps me up at night is how to hold onto these lessons and experiences and not take myself so seriously. It's easy to let the glow of extraordinary experiences fade as routine takes over, but I'm determined that this journey won't simply become a fond memory. Instead, it marks a turning point—an opportunity to live more intentionally. We've returned with a deeper appreciation for life beyond work and material success, seeing the true value in creating lasting memories with our children, teaching them to be curious and adventurous, and fostering what we call 'failure immunity'. We defined it as the ability to face setbacks without letting them define you, replacing the weight of feeling like a failure with resilience, humor, and growth.

I experienced this firsthand upon returning home. The fear of losing my job had once seemed like the ultimate failure. Yet when I discovered my position was no longer available, what initially felt like a setback became a catalyst for change. Without this push, I might never have pursued writing this book or would have let the dream fade into someday. Even the act of writing itself required embracing potential failure–opening myself up to criticism with my first book. But our journey had taught me that the greatest risks often lead to the most meaningful rewards.

During my travels, I encountered a tale that beautifully captures what it means to develop failure immunity. In a small village in northern Thailand, locals have a clever way of catching monkeys. They chain a clay jug with a narrow neck to a tree and place treats inside. A monkey, drawn by the scent, slips its hand through the narrow opening to grab the food. But once its fist is clenched around the treasure, it becomes too big to pull back through the opening. Trapped, the monkey panics and struggles, unwilling to let go of the prize, even as danger approaches.

I realized I had often been that monkey—trapped not by circumstances but by my fear of failure and the shame of letting go. For years, I clung to an idea of success that left no room for mistakes, afraid to release my grip on what wasn't working. But watching my kids explore the world taught me something transformative: failure is inevitable, but it doesn't have to define you. Letting go of the fear of feeling like a failure is the first step toward freedom and growth. True resilience lies not in avoiding failure but in refusing to let it trap you.

This understanding has manifested in unexpected ways since our return to Toronto. When I discovered my position was no longer available upon our return, my initial instinct was to dive straight into the job search — and I did. But something had shifted within me. After crunching the numbers with our family budget, we realized there was an opportunity to explore a different path. I could dedicate time to writing, public speaking, and volunteering for causes close to my heart, particularly promoting literacy for young kids. Everything happens for a reason, and I now feel invigorated by what this next chapter might look like. I'm more purposeful about how I spend my time, rediscovering old passions

I'd set aside years ago. Golf, which I hadn't played since my early twenties, has become both a meditative escape and a humbling reminder that it's never too late to restart something you love–even if my swing isn't quite as consistent as I'd like to pretend it is.

The kids, too, have carried forward pieces of our journey in unexpected ways. Ayana, inspired by the games of Bedouin chess she witnessed during our travels, delightedly took up chess at school, building on that spark of interest. Both she and Kasia have branched beyond their usual basketball routines into cross-country running, waking earlier than ever with surprising enthusiasm. Ayana is especially excited about trying out for her first school team, perhaps inspired by her namesake — Almaz Ayana, the Ethiopian runner who shattered the women's 10,000m world record at the 2016 Olympics. Kasia recently competed in Toronto's cross-country city finals and has seamlessly transitioned to her new school, diving into sports I hadn't even heard of, like bordenball and soccer cricket.

Meanwhile, Janice is thriving in her new role at work, where the adaptability she honed during our travels shines through. Our home now features pieces of art from each country we visited, daily reminders of the places that shaped our perspectives. While we considered extending our time abroad, we recognized that returning to school for the kids and being closer to our aging parents was the right decision for now. Nothing is forever, but every choice can be right for its moment.

Perhaps the greatest lesson from this experience has been understanding that we don't have to settle. Other cultures embrace life with refreshing passion, connection, and appreciation for the present moment. In contrast, many of us endure life, caught in routines that rarely bring lasting joy. Our time away showed us there's another way — we don't have to wait for retirement to start living the life we dream about.

As we look to the future, we do so knowing that this journey was just the beginning. Like that monkey in northern Thailand, we all face moments when we must choose between holding onto what's familiar or embracing the unknown. The world is waiting, not just to be explored, but to show you versions of yourself you never knew existed. Here's to your next adventure— may it bring you closer to the life you're meant to live.

Key Takeaways

1. The Power of Letting Go: True freedom and growth come not from holding tight to what's familiar, but from having the courage to release our grip on routines, expectations, and perceived security.

2. Living Intentionally: Life's richest experiences don't require waiting for retirement or the "right moment"—they begin when we choose to live purposefully in the present, finding joy in both planned and unexpected moments.

3. Universal Connection: Despite cultural and geographical differences, people everywhere share the same fundamental desires: to build better lives, find joy in small moments, and explore the world with curiosity.

Key Questions

1. What would you dare to pursue if you knew that struggle and uncertainty were not signs of weakness, but stepping stones to growth?

2. How might your daily life change if you stopped enduring moments and started experiencing them, just as other cultures do?

3. What 'clay pot' are you holding onto right now - what comfort, belief, or habit - that might actually be holding you back from a more authentic life?

PAUSE AND REFLECT: Your Journey Begins

1. Let Go of Control

   TODAY: Notice where you're gripping too tightly – maybe it's your daily schedule, your career path, or even your self-image. Take one small step to loosen that grip.

   THIS WEEK: Put yourself in a situation that makes you uncomfortable – join an improv class, take a solo dinner at a restaurant, or strike up a conversation with a stranger.

   THIS MONTH: Plan a family adventure that pushes everyone's comfort zones – maybe it's camping if you're city folks, or exploring a culture completely different from your own.

2. Live with Purpose

   - Challenge yourself to say "no" to one commitment that doesn't align with your values

   - Create a morning ritual that's just for you, before the world makes its demands

   - Identify one area of your life where you're living by someone else's rules and reimagine it

3. Create Lasting Impact

   - Start a project you've been putting off, even if you don't feel ready

   - Share your dreams with someone who might help make them reality

   - Take one step toward changing the part of your life story you've been wanting to rewrite

APPENDIX
TIPS & RECOMMENDATIONS

"Travel is the only thing you buy that makes you richer."
- Anonymous

Travelling around the world with my family taught us many valuable lessons, from the practicalities of managing luggage to the transformative practice of making the most of every moment. Below, I've compiled some of the most useful tips and recommendations that made our journey smoother and more enjoyable. Whether you're planning a weekend getaway or a year-long adventure, these insights might just make your trip a little easier.

Essential Travel Tips

1. Document Your Luggage: Before you even set foot in an airport, take a moment to snap pictures of your suitcases, including any carry-on bags. If your luggage gets lost, these photos can be invaluable when reporting it to the airline. Trust me, the stress of losing luggage is bad enough—having photos ready can speed up the recovery process.

2. Reusable Bags Are a Must: We found that bringing along two reusable bags was a lifesaver. Whether we were grocery shopping or just needed an extra bag for miscellaneous items, these bags were incredibly handy. They fold up easily, take up minimal space, and are eco-friendly—a win-win!

3. Digital Cameras for the Kids: We gave each of our daughters a cheap digital camera so they could create their own photo journal of the trip. It was far more useful—and entertaining—than letting them use our iPhone cameras. They captured moments through their own eyes, choosing what to remember and document. Watching them excitedly snap photos gave them a sense of ownership in the journey and provided us with some surprising gems of the trip that we might have otherwise missed!

4. GuideGeek for Tailored Advice: When the internet became overwhelming with choices, GuideGeek on WhatsApp was our go-to. We could ask specific questions about what to do, eat, and see or where to sleep and get tailored responses. It was like having a personal guide at our fingertips.

5. Withlocals.com: Our love for food led us to explore cities through the lens of local cuisine, and Withlocals.com became our go-to for this experience. In four different countries, we joined food tours guided by locals who not only took us to hidden restaurants and vibrant markets but also shared the rich history and culture of their cities. These tours allowed us to connect with each place on a deeper level, turning every meal into a memorable cultural exchange. Watching our daughters eagerly try new dishes and learn the stories behind them was a highlight of our trip, making these food tours a cornerstone of our travel experience.

6. Currency Conversion Made Easy: Using the Scotiabank Passport Infinite credit card was a game-changer for our travels. We negotiated with the bank to have the annual fee waived for the first year to test it out, and it quickly became our go-to for international purchases. Each time we made a purchase, we received an email detailing the cost in

Canadian dollars, helping us stay on track with our budget. A great bonus was the card's inclusion of six complimentary lounge passes, which were incredibly useful during our trip. Additionally, the card waived foreign transaction fees, making purchases more affordable.

7. WISE Accounts for Easy Cash Access: WISE accounts were our backup plan for countries that didn't widely accept credit cards. Linked to our Canadian bank account, we could easily convert money to local currencies with minimal fees. We used it sparingly, but it was a relief to know we had cash on hand when needed.

Technology and Connectivity

8. Facebook Groups for Families: Janice found incredible value in joining groups for families travelling with kids to destinations on our itinerary. These groups offered support, discount codes, and curated lists of activities that became invaluable resources. In countries like Thailand and the Philippines, where many local events and activities lacked dedicated websites but maintained active Facebook pages, these groups helped us discover experiences we might have otherwise overlooked.

9. Airline Apps for Peace of Mind: Having airline apps on our phones was a no-brainer. We received alerts about delays, gate changes, and flight cancellations well in advance. While email notifications are helpful, the apps kept us one step ahead, which was crucial when taking 30+ flights.

10. E-SIM Seamless Connectivity: Internet access and connectivity can be major concerns while travelling. Enter Airalo, an e-SIM card that allowed us to purchase data packages for different countries or regions right from our phones. This meant we could connect to a local network as soon as we landed in a new country, avoiding the hassle of buying SIM cards at each airport or buying an expensive roaming package from our Canadian cell phone provider. It was seamless and worked like a charm, and it's one of those things that I am surprised more people are not aware of or use when travelling internationally.

Transportation and Accommodation

11. Hop-on Hop-off Buses: When time was tight, or we wanted to get a quick overview of a city, Hop-on Hop-off buses were the way to go. They helped us cover a lot of ground without getting overwhelmed and allowed us to decide which sites to explore in more depth. In cities like Johannesburg, where safety can be a concern, these buses also provided a secure way to see the sights. Holding on to our receipts enabled us to receive future discounts in other cities where this option was available.

12. Airbnb and Booking.com: A large majority of our stays were in Airbnbs, which gave us the comfort and flexibility we needed, especially as a family. I only wish they had a loyalty program—we would have racked up major points! For the remaining 20%, we used Booking.com or opted for unique stays. Staying in Airbnbs rather than hotels also allowed us to connect with the country on a deeper level. Each stay gave us a glimpse into the local way of life and tips about the best local spots to avoid tourist traps.

13. Local Transportation Apps: Before arriving in each major city, we downloaded their local transportation apps (like Grab in Southeast Asia). Having these ready to go meant we could avoid tourist pricing for taxis and navigate like locals from the moment we landed. Plus, the ability to input destinations in English while the driver saw them in the local language eliminated many communication barriers.

Money-Saving Strategies While Travelling

Planning and budgeting were central to making our around-the-world trip a reality. Through careful consideration and strategic choices, we found ways to maximize our savings while still enjoying the journey to its fullest. Here's how we approached saving money during our travels:

1. Packing Light to Minimize Costs: One of the first decisions we made was to pack light, bringing only carry-ons and a suitcase each. This allowed us to avoid hefty baggage fees, simplify travel between destinations, and streamline our airport experience by skipping baggage claim. It also made our transitions quicker and less stressful, which proved invaluable when navigating tight connections or multiple stops in different countries.

2. Booking Major Activities in Advance: Advance booking of major activities turned out to be a significant cost-saving strategy. For instance, we secured our safari stay at the Honeyguide Khoka Moya Camp in South Africa well ahead of time. This not only ensured our spot at a popular destination but also came with a perk—an additional free night's stay when booking for three nights. By planning these big-ticket activities early, we could lock in better rates and build the rest of our itinerary around them with confidence.

3. Timing Visits for Savings: Another key strategy was timing our visits to align with off-peak seasons or periods when we could save on expenses. Our trip to the Great Barrier Reef is a perfect example. We planned our visit for late February to early March, right as the school year began in Australia. This choice meant we benefited from lower rates and a less crowded experience. The large boat that took us to the reef was practically empty, making for a more relaxed and enjoyable outing.

4. Meal Planning for Cost Efficiency: Managing our meals thoughtfully also made a significant difference in our budget. Most days, we prepared breakfast at our accommodation when it wasn't provided, sticking to simple, affordable items that were easy to make. For lunch, we often had sandwiches, keeping things light and efficient so we could continue exploring without the expense of dining out. Dinner was usually our splurge, giving us the opportunity to enjoy local cuisine and desserts while experiencing the cultural atmosphere of each place.

This approach varied depending on the country. In destinations like Thailand and the Philippines, where dining out was inexpensive due to a strong restaurant/market culture, it was actually cheaper to eat all our meals at local eateries. We delighted in trying street food and modest restaurants, which added to the authenticity of our trip. Conversely, in higher-cost destinations like Australia and New Zealand, we stuck to our plan of home-cooked breakfasts and lunches, saving dinner as our main dining experience.

5. Benefiting from a Strong Exchange Rate: A significant financial advantage throughout our journey was the strength of the Canadian dollar in many of the countries we visited. This exchange rate gave us stronger purchasing power, making it more affordable to buy goods, pay for activities, and enjoy local services. The favourable currency conversion stretched our budget further than we initially expected, allowing us to make the most of our experience without constant financial worry.

Key Takeaways

1. Efficient Travel Planning: Packing light and booking major activities in advance saves money and reduces stress, allowing for smoother travel experiences.

2. Smart Budgeting: Using tools like Scotiabank Passport Infinite and WISE accounts helps manage currency conversion, while meal planning and timing visits with off-peak seasons maximize savings.

3. Cultural Immersion: Engaging in local food tours and encouraging kids to document their journey adds authenticity to your travel experience and creates lasting memories.

ACKNOWLEDGEMENTS

Every story begins somewhere, and mine was shaped by extraordinary teachers who saw potential in a young boy. To Melodie, Ms. McWhinnie, Ms. Dodgson, Ms. Karsh, Mrs. MacDonald and Mr. Callaghan—your guidance and encouragement laid the foundation for who I would become. You taught me more than just lessons; you showed me how to believe in myself.

To Jackie, Joyce, Christine and Michaela—being your sibling has been one of my greatest joys (even when you all ganged up on me). Your pride in this journey means everything to me, though I know you'll never let it go to my head.

To my Ghanaian family—from cousins in Ottawa to my extended community in Ghana and around the world: it takes a village, and you've been mine. You anchor me to my roots even as you help me fly.

To Ron and Cathy, and the entire Saskatchewan family—you welcomed me with open arms and open hearts, showing me that love knows no bounds. Your warmth, laughter, and endless support have made me feel like I've always belonged. Though you do occasionally remind me that I married your favourite child....

To my band of misfit friends who somehow became family—thanks for being there for both the sensible dreams and the crazy schemes, and for knowing exactly when I needed either one.

A special thank you to Samantha and Samar and the Lucky Book Publishing team, who saw something in these pages that I couldn't yet see. Your unwavering faith in my story and gentle push helped me find my voice when I doubted myself.

Finally, to the universe that conspired to make this journey possible—thank you for showing me that our greatest stories often lie in our most ordinary moments.

ABOUT THE AUTHOR

Charles Achampong inspires others to embrace the present and reconnect with what truly matters. With over 20 years of experience across the public, private, philanthropic, and non-profit sectors, he has dedicated his career to empowering communities. A life-changing journey around the world with his family shifted his perspective, teaching him to replace future anxieties with gratitude for everyday moments. Charles now shares his insights through writing and speaking, helping individuals and families prioritize connection, mindfulness, and intentional living. His work encourages readers to pause, reflect, and uncover what brings meaning and fulfillment to their lives. He lives in Toronto with his wife and two kids.

Instagram: @aroundtheworldinfamilydays
LinkedIn: https://www.linkedin.com/in/
            charlesachampong
Website: https://www.charlesachampong.com
Email: info@charlesachampong.com

thank you

Thank you for reading my book!

Dear Reader,

You made it! Thanks for sticking with me through these pages. I hope they brought you some insights, a few laughs, and maybe even a spark of inspiration. Sharing these stories and lessons has been an incredible journey, and it means a lot that you chose to be a part of it.

Now, if I could ask a quick favour: if you enjoyed the book, would you mind leaving a positive review on Amazon or Goodreads? It would truly make my day, and it's one of the best ways to help others find this book and maybe spark their own adventure. Your review might just be the encouragement someone else needs to give them permission to break from routine and empower them to make the change they need.

Best,
Charles

MY GIFT TO YOU

I am so glad you're here!

As my Gift to you, get FREE Access to the Audiobook of
Around the World in Family Days
by scanning the QR Code below or visiting
https://www.charlesachampong.com/thebook